FROM THE SAME WRITER

The Wit and Wisdom of an Ordinary Subject (2013)

More Wit and Wisdom of an Ordinary Subject (2014)

Yet More Wit and Wisdom of an Ordinary Subject

Malcolm Watson

Soldier, Cricketer, Man of Letters

First published April 2016 using Lulu.com

Fist Revise

ISBN 978-1-326-56374-5

In memory of the late Nicky Till,
a friend since prep school days and
a great supporter of my efforts in print,
who died on 12 February 2016.

FOREWORDS

Soldier

When Malcolm worked for me 35 years ago
(although it sometimes seemed the other way
round), I remember reporting that he wrote clearly
and well. I had not expected this talent to lead to
three volumes of letters, but what a pleasure it has
been to catch some of them in the press, read the
books and yet more here, knowing the twinkle in the
eye that lies behind them. One of a generation of
servicemen who saw that the Cold War was won (and
whose tale has still to be told), his keen idiosyncratic
observations on life and travel at home and abroad
will surely extend into *Even More Wit and Wisdom....* of
a far from ordinary subject.

General Sir Garry Johnson KCB OBE MC
Commander-in Chief Allied Forces Northern Europe
1992 - 1994

Cricketer

As you would expect of a Yorkshireman, Malcolm
tells it like it is. His range is broad, his aim true and
very little escapes his notice or his (occasionally
friendly) fire. Dotted in amongst the other letters and
comments are commentaries on our great game from
the village green to the Test arena – whether it be the

closure of club cricket grounds, Kevin Pietersen's tattoos or memories of playing in Kenya, the entries are by turn warm, revealing and entertaining.

Matt Thacker
Managing Editor, *The Nightwatchman*
The *Wisden* Cricket Quarterly

Man of Letters

Newspapers receive dozens of letters from readers each day but few are as attentive and as concise in their writing as Malcolm. As a regular contributor to the *Evening Standard,* he ranges between the political and comical in his letters and is simply a delight to read. His writing provides a crucial reminder to our journalists that accuracy in their reports is essential and even fellow correspondents will not get away with incorrect assertions. This latest volume provides many more moments of laughter and controversy for the readers - and embarrassment for the writers and editors he has rightfully called out.

Joe Krishnan
Letters Editor of the *Evening Standard*

April 2016

CONTENTS

INTRODUCTION

This third volume, coming a further eighteen months after the second (*More Wit and Wisdom of an Ordinary Subject*), continues its format with a Travel section offering further tips and recommendations to the *Telegraph* newspapers' travel sections and another, Extras, for additional submissions and correspondence. So here are yet more published letters and other items, along with many more that weren't, which is the real core of this book.

The main recipients continue to be the *Times* and *Telegraph* newspapers followed by the *Evening Standard*. This collection also contains debut letters published in *The Spectator, The Independent, The Sunday Times, Culture* section, as well as *The Lady* and *Cigar Aficionado*.

On 25th February 2016, the date *The Daily Telegraph* published its 50,000th edition, the editor of the letters page went onto the *Today* programme on Radio 4. He mentioned that they have a rule of thumb not to publish the same person more than once a month. At the time, I had already had two published in February, but managed to leap over him with a third one on the 29th!

As to clues to content that will attract the eyes of editors of letters pages: in the case of *The Times*, in addition to succinctness and courtesy, I find that their description of "interesting is good, quirkiness is better and humour is best of all when we need to fill an awkward hole in the jigsaw" remains valid guidance;

and I continue to be guided by advice that *The Daily Telegraph* letters page, as well as being about important things, also specialises in "whimsy and wry observations about daily life".

I hope you find that at least some of these latest offerings meet these criteria.

Malcolm Watson

Welford
Berkshire

April 2016

PREFACE

Published letters that follow are in a larger font to distinguish them from the others which were unpublished and are in a smaller font. Both have the subject heading in bold.

The letters, or other submissions, are shown in date order as a reminder of some of the issues of the day. The dates shown are the date of publication, or the date of submission for those not published. Dates shown as references are in the format used in each publication.

The titles *The Daily Telegraph* and *The Sunday Telegraph* have been abbreviated to *DTel* and *STel* for unpublished letters and the definite article dropped for published letters to save space. Salutations, where they appear, are as used in the individual publications.

All letters have been signed: Malcolm Watson, Welford, Berkshire, except to the *Evening Standard* which are signed J M C Watson, or as shown.

Rank has only been used when writing on military matters to give credibility to the points being made.

Letters published in *The Times* under the leading subject of the day are no longer shown in bold type or accompanied by a picture. At around the same time, those published in the *Telegraph* newspapers with the picture came to be shown in bold, except where the picture accompanies the leading subject of the day. The changes are reflected here, where letters published with a picture have (P) after the title. In all cases, the actual title of published letters is used and will be that for the group of letters, when there was more than one. Where there was no title for letters published in the *Evening Standard*, the one in brackets was used for its submission.

Where some letters seem to be repeated at later dates, they have been included to demonstrate the determination to get the subject aired, or share the wit. When such letters were sent to different publications on roughly the same dates, they are shown together as a single entry.

Entries in italics are from other sources, for material edited out, or for notes by way of explanation.

WHERE WE LEFT OFF

Take applause together

During an otherwise uneven contest in the recent Royal London match between Hampshire and Yorkshire at the Ageas Bowl, Jimmy Adams with 91 not out and Adil Rashid with 5 for 35 were rightly clapped from the field as the first innings ended.

However, they left it yards apart through separate gates, effectively splitting the crowd's applause, instead of through a single gate with the batsman leading the bowler off, to deserved applause from the fielders as well. I was told that this is what the players want; but they left through the batting side's gate at the end of the game after the handshakes and children provided a guard of honour at the start.

Thus respect for your opponents takes a further knock. I am not convinced that the players should have their way there.

Daily Telegraph   29 Aug 14

Devastated, indeed, by the over-use of words

SIR - The increasing misuse of *sustainable* is not sustainable.

Country Life   3 Sep 14

The soldier's lexicon

Mark Lindesay is right about officer cadets using CLAP at Sandhurst (*Letters, August 13*), which was not solely put to use on the parade ground. On the noisy battlefield they also had to remember the sequence GRIT (Group, Range, Indication, and Type of fire) before giving orders to troops to open fire - Clearly, Loudly, As an order, and with Pauses.   Above all, KISS reminded us that the best plan was often an uncomplicated plan - Keep It Simple, Stupid.
J. M. C. Watson, Berkshire

| *The Times* | **Challenger bank** | 4 Sep 14 |

Sir, Your Business section today (page 48) has the strange juxtaposition of a military vehicle, which is apparently a "tank" but without a gun, opposite a report about a "challenger*", which is a bank without any branches.

*A *tank, which does have a gun.*

| *DTel* | **New sperm bank** | 24 Sep 14 |

SIR - I heard by chance on Radio 4's *Woman's Hour* this week that the first National Sperm Bank in Birmingham aims to boost the number of "men" donors wishing to sign up. Though restricted to those between 20 and 40 years of age, it must be a relief for all concerned that the woman's hour has not yet cometh.

2014

Daily Telegraph   1 Oct

Scoff between stops

SIR - Darren Johnson, a Green member of
the London Assembly, extols the virtues of
travelling by bus (Letters, September 22).
Unfortunately, less sociable habits such as
eating, and sharing, takeaway meals - at any
time of day or night - seem to have
accompanied the 64 per cent increase in bus
passenger trips being undertaken there.

It would be a joy to visitors from the rest
of the country if Mr Johnson used his
influence to address this unwelcome
development.

*Mr Johnson had written that it would be a joy to reward
commuters in the rest of the country with a world-class bus
network and a Dutch-style cycling infrastructure. For
subsequent correspondence go to pages 182 and 183.*

The Times   **Mountain heights**   1 Oct

Sir, Given that mountaineer Haversham Godwin-
Austen lived from 1834 to 1923 (letter, Oct 1), I expect
that his world high-altitude summiting record

(6,250m) was known as 20,505ft (3in) – just as for many of us, the height of Mount Everest will always be 29,002ft and not what it is in metres.

Evening Standard **Income tax thresholds** 2 Oct

Jolyon Maughan (letter, Thurs) is being disingenuous when he says that if you earn less than £10,500 you won't benefit at all from David Cameron's headline measure of raising the income tax threshold to £12,500. Of course you won't: if you don't pay income tax in the first place, you can't benefit from a cut in it.

Equally disingenuous is his question "What have you done to lift people out of poverty?" when coupled with the answer "I raised the personal allowance to £12,500"; which as a specialist tax barrister he will know only too well.

The Times **Yet another pill** 5 Oct

Sir, What, another pill for goodness sake? Get me a drink. ("Pill is not miracle cure in the battle to help alcoholics ", Oct 4).

A new pill was recommended for those succumbing to two glasses of wine a night.

The Times **Bankers free to leave** 10 Oct

Sir, Sometimes, fundamental freedoms need forfeiting for the greater good. Reversing the burden of proof for bankers suspected of reckless misconduct is not without precedent (letter, Oct 10): in the 1970s, endemic corruption in the public service in Hong Kong, still then a Crown Colony, was tackled this way. Appeals against the 1970 Prevention of Bribery Ordinance, on grounds of jurisdiction and against conviction, went all the way to the Judicial Committee of the Privy Council and both failed. Messrs Trueman and Johnson, resigning as directors of HSBC, would seem to be wise to 'jump the gun'.

DTel **For all the people** 11 Oct

SIR - Nicholas Wightwick is mistaken in saying that when seats are won with 40 per cent of the vote "this leaves 60 per cent unrepresented" (Letters, October 11). An MP returned to Parliament represents not only all those who voted but, equally important, the many who didn't vote at all, and for whatever reason. In spite of some disenchantment with them, MPs can still be relied upon to represent all their constituents, in leafy glade or seaside town, regardless of political complexion or none.

DTel　　　　　**Draught Clooney**　　　　14 Oct

SIR - With her family connections there, Bryony
Gordon would seem to have plenty of opportunity
and a good chance of seeing George Clooney in the
pub in Sonning, but not of getting the pint of
Brakspear she asks him for (Features, October 14) - it's
a Fuller's pub.

The Spectator　　　　　　　　　　**18 Oct**

In defence of KP

Sir: Peter Oborne is right that some of Kevin
Pietersen's most brilliant innings in world
cricket over the last ten years will stay with
cricket lovers for ever ('An excess of spin',
11 October), but wrong that his
autobiography, *KP*, won't. The vivid prose
has lifted the lid on what has been said in
the dressing room and questioned the adage
that what is said there should remain there.
As Pietersen puts it, 'There was a story that
had to be told'; cutting against the spin,
there is also a case to answer. What comes
over most clearly is that any enjoyment had

gone out of playing for England. Pietersen may best be served by a period of silence on his part, while a new chief executive of the ECB takes up the post. I'm not betting on the silence, but something better must surely emerge for players and cricket lovers alike. The book will stay among my cricket books, alphabetically by author, alongside Oborne's brilliant *Basil D'Oliveira* (2004) for as long as I have them; to be joined, I hope, by future memoirs of players whose joy at playing for this country is once again palpable and for whom some fun is restored to touring abroad.

The Times   **Robotic help**   18 Oct

Sir, Just how far we still have to go in humanoid robotics was well illustrated 25 years ago when I heard a leading scientist explain that a robot his grandson hoped for, to play table tennis against, was still a very long way off. The appearance of the most advanced creation, with football skills ("Lonely in old age? Not with a caring robot", Oct 18), demonstrates some progress; it may also explain in part why children embrace the vision and British adults seem not to. But never mind the handling of champagne flutes and the best china, what would really help the elderly is a reduction in the high cost of riser/recliner chairs.

The Times **Save us from the spads** 19 Oct

Sir, Congratulations to Rishi Sunak, a businessman, on being selected as the Conservative parliamentary candidate for William Hague's constituency of Richmond (Yorks). How encouraging it was, though, to read that two special advisers (Theresa May's) did not make the short list (Westminster Diary, Oct 18).

Daily Mail **Buck's Fizz** 22 Oct

It was not "in the Eighties when it was thought chic to mix champagne with orange juice to make Buck's Fizz" as stated by Jilly Goolden (life, Oct 21), but in the Twenties when it was invented at Buck's Club in London as an excuse to begin drinking early. It was the pop group Bucks Fizz, which achieved success in the Eighties, when Jilly was charming us on BBC2's Food and Drink programme with her outrageously abstract descriptions of wine.

The Times   **Correcting mistakes**   22 Oct
Feedback

Robin Rhoderick-Jones's informative letter (Model
Africa) on Wednesday referred to Richard Lloyd
Parry (Opinion, Tuesday) wrongly grouping
Botswana with North Korea, Cuba and Iran as pariah
states. However, the mistake had been corrected to
Zimbabwe online before the letter was posted there
on Tuesday evening. What are the criteria for a letter
pointing out an error, over the publication of a
correction, or vice versa? A correction would still
seem to be desirable in this case as the letter did not
go as far as saying that the country should have been
Zimbabwe.

The Oldie   **And the winner is....**   23 Oct

SIR: I wonder if I am alone in seeing in the winning
entry for the 2014 Oldie British Artists Award
(November issue) a herd of elephants crossing the
path of the monster emerging from Loch Ness; or,
regarding the description of the painting on behalf of
the panel of judges, an obvious candidate for Pseuds
Corner in *Private Eye*. What on earth are they all on?

Evening Standard   **Tesco**   23 Oct

Your Business Connections advertisement for Sir Terry Leahy, ex chief executive of Tesco Ltd, to talk about "How to innovate and take your business to the next level" might attract more attendees if it was reworded as "How to restore your business to its former level" (News and Business, Thurs); but then maybe not.

The Times   **Head-to-head finish**   23 Oct

Sir, The need for "point-to-point airports" (letters, Oct 24) has a ring of the film *Those Magnificent Men in their Flying Machines* (1965) about it: sharing the glory and the prize – now between Heathrow and Gatwick – may yet be a fitting ending to the airport capacity conundrum.

Evening Standard   24 Oct

(Woolf whistle)

The practice of appointing inquiry chiefs from the roll call of the great and the good is due an overhaul: the great all know each other and the good are not limited to those who are great. Lord Mayor Fiona Woolf should stand down and a good candidate be selected with experience, knowledge and potential to achieve greatness by completing the task.

Mrs Woolf stood down a week later.

The Times   **Sleepy Wilton**   27 Oct

SIR - The Mayor of Wilton, the town near Salisbury, puts the record straight about its provenance and vibrancy (letter, Oct 27). There is, though, a small village called Wilton in Wiltshire, near the Kennet & Avon Canal and the only working windmill in the county, which might even be proud to be described as sleepy.

DTel   **Royal visit to Columbia**   1 Nov

SIR - It is disappointing that The Prince of Wales and The Duchess of Cornwall did not have time during their four-day visit to Columbia to find out how £15 million is being spent there over four years by the Department of Energy and Climate Change to monitor flatulent cows and reduce greenhouse gas emissions from cattle ranching (Report, February 17). Let's just hope it isn't all disappearing into thick air.

The Spectator   **Dropping titles – and the ball**   1 Nov

Sir: Sir Peregrine Worsthorne was knighted as long ago as 1991 (letter, 1 November). It has become the fashion for some publishers and writers not to use titles, though I suspect that it wasn't the writer in this case.

The Times   **Head this way**   2 Nov

Sir, Instead of drawing up another list of possible contenders to approach, let the Home Office, in conjunction with the victims' representatives, draw up a specification for the person to head the child sex abuse inquiry and invite applications. They may be surprised to find that there will be some excellent people out there, with the knowledge, experience and potential to get it right and complete the task. Give them the opportunity to do so and select the best.

The Times   **Luggage-only flights**   6 Nov

Sir, So that's why Miami Airport is full of travellers with huge bundles of shrink-wrapped personal belongings: passenger flights to and from Central and South America simply can't be carrying freight in their belly-holds (letter, Nov 6).

Evening Standard   **Donuts**   6 Nov

Surely doughnut not donut (Texts, Wed); or this
paper for London, Ohio or Kentucky?

DTel   **EAW surprises**   6 Nov

SIR - Your front page report (November 6) misquotes
the letter from some of Britain's senior legal figures
about the European Arrest Warrant:
"[Unsurprisingly,] the Association of Chief Police
Officers believes we cannot afford to lose it." What is
surprising is that such weight is given to the view of
an organisation which we can apparently afford to
lose.

Evening Standard   7 Nov

(Links with WW1)

I am a generation younger than General
Beach (Wed) so my link with the 1914-1918
war is through my grandfather losing his
brother and my grandmother three
brothers. The reason I went to visit the
poppies at the Tower is best explained by
the wording at the end of the memorial

scroll sent to next of kin: "Let those that come after see to it that his name be not forgotten." Their names are now known to my own family, who have also visited.
Col (retired) J M C Watson

DTel **Archers unheard** 9 Nov

SIR - I don't listen to *The Archers*, but never miss the correspondence about it. Keep it coming, whatever the storyline.

DTel **Other sobriquets** 9 Nov

SIR - I have heard residents of the Isle of Wight refer to mainland Britain as the North Island.

Sunday Times 9 Nov
Culture section

(Downton shockers*)

Seeing the sign outside the tea room Betty's with the apostrophe missing, decades before it was rebranded without one, was much more shocking than seeing Lord Grantham in a fight.

*Also included Mr Moseley's shirt front, but see below)

Independent	**The Berlin Wall**	10 Nov

The line of balloons to celebrate the 25th anniversary of the fall of the Berlin Wall did not mark a 15km stretch of the former "Iron Curtain" (News, November 10), but of the former Wall, though it did symbolize it. The "Iron Curtain" ran in part between East and West Germany passing some 170km to the west of Berlin. Also, it should not be forgotten that the Wall ran for 43km roughly north-south, cleaving Berlin in two, and for another 112km isolating the enclave of West Berlin from the surrounding East German state, preventing East Germans from fleeing communism.

The Times   14 Nov

Tuxedo collars

Sir, Given all the correspondence about detachable collars, it must have been easy to miss the starched shirt fronts in *Downton Abbey*: Mr Moseley wore his done up the wrong way - like a lady's blouse - throughout the last series.

Evening Standard **Legal niceties** 17 Nov

By John Slinger's logic about barbaric methods of killing (letter, Mon), presumably we should regard those "hanged, drawn and quartered" merely to have been subject to "the law's full sanction".

The Times **Jammy dodgers** 20 Nov

Sir, My father, now 94, was interested to hear of the award of the Legion d'Honneur to living veterans of the Normandy Landings (News, 18 Nov and letter, Nov 20). As a veteran of the Italian Campaign, he has been used to the aspersion of being a "D-day dodger". Fortunately, he was much amused when I offered him some jam filled biscuits by way of consolation.

Country Life **Digital hygiene** 20 Nov

Michael Brook is perhaps being a little overdramatic about the future availability of hard-copy COUNTRY LIFEs in drawing rooms throughout the civilised world (Letter, November 12); we can certainly expect them to be there for the foreseeable future. But in waiting rooms, donated copies are already getting scarcer as more and more surgeries turn magazines down, not just for lifestyle reasons such as the *Shooting Times* and *Cigar Aficionado*, but for fear of infection. I already subscribe to three national magazines and can access them all on my smart phone while waiting for the doctor or dentist, for no additional subscription. The welcome decision to include full digital access with your Christmas subscription offer has made it irresistible. Though the magazine is a gift for my wife, I shall look forward to reading it on my phone in waiting rooms, wherever in the world they may be.

DTel	**Wrong sort of ban**	21 Nov

SIR - Perhaps Sam Kirkaldy means a ban on sachets being used for sauces (Letters, November 21). If all sauces produced in sachets were banned, they wouldn't be available in jars or bottles either.

Sunday Times *Sport section*	**(Sport letters)**	23 Nov

The England rugby team's performances won't be transformed by eliminating mistakes. Only by developing flair can they hope to win the World Cup.

DTel	**Hanging on**	25 Nov

SIR - Peter Willoughby omitted from his analogy with Ukip that Liberal Eric Lubbock held onto his Orpington seat in the General Elections of 1964 and 1966 before the Conservatives regained it 1970 (Letters, November 25). The hung parliament in 1964 that led to an early election in 1966 is also a possible scenario for 2015, early elections still being allowed under the Fixed-term Parliaments Act 2011.

The Times	**Last straw**	26 Nov

Sir, I now associate the words "for ever and ever, Amen" with each call for surgeons to take more responsibility for the safe recovery of their patients (letters, Nov 26). Health Minister Sir Bruce Keogh is right to require surgeons' death rates to be published: they might then review their collective practices and code of ethics, including being part of, or even leading, the health team assigned to their patients and for which the skill of the surgeon is a factor in the team's success (letter, Nov 21).

Evening Standard 26 Nov

(The Oldie)

Never mind getting Richard Ingrams back
to The Oldie as a columnist (Wed) - we
want him back as the editor.
J M C Watson, Oldie subscriber (still)

The Spectator 29 Nov

The Army went first

Sir: May I correct the assertion that the
cricket tour of Pakistan by a team made up,
largely, of elderly white blokes from
London, including Roger Alton (Sport,
November 15), was the first to tour the
country since the appalling terrorist attack
there on the Sri Lankans in 2009. The Army
team, made up entirely of youthful soldiers,
toured there at the end of 2012. According
to the BBC, they received rave reviews and
had all their matches broadcast live on national television. *Col J.M.C.Watson (retired)*

DTel   **Other uses of Marigolds**   28 Nov

SIR - I try to keep my attempts at washing up well on the right side of rare but have never felt the need to use gloves (Letters, November 28); though I have found man-size Marigolds useful for clearing gutters and drains.

Sunday Telegraph   30 Nov

Downton discrepancies, from etiquette to fashion (P)

SIR - I was surprised to read that Alistair Bruce, a historical adviser on *Downton Abbey*, is a lieutenant colonel in the Army Reserve. I gather that the wearing of Sam Browne belts - from the positioning of the belt buckle to their being worn indoors – has been the most frequently criticised detail of accuracy in this popular costume drama.

I sympathise with Mr Bruce's predicament over "men in tights", but a real stickler would never have let improper

dressing hold sway over looking good.
Col J M C Watson (rtd)

DTel   **Mocktails**   1 Dec

SIR - I fear that Julia Bishop is likely to find the names of non-alcoholic drinks more exciting than the drinks themselves (letters, Dec 1). But what a Boo Boo's Special, a Jersey Lillie and a Surfer's Paradise have in common is a dash of Angostura Bitters to perk them up. For tomato juice based drinks it is celery salt that provides the excitement.

The Times   **Driving lessons for the elderly**   3 Dec

Sir, The ability of elderly people to drive a car is governed by long-term memory (letter, Dec 3); the success for them of an annual lesson with a certified instructor would depend on the state of their short-term memory. Remembering safer driving techniques which were successfully practised during a lesson is likely to be as difficult, for some, as remembering where they have parked. Getting them to give up their licences is best left to families, who must not shirk their responsibilities when helping them to comply with the existing system of validation.

| *DTel* | **Havana** | 4 Dec |

SIR - With only 36 hours to spend in Havana (Travel, December 3), a small adjustment could still be made to include the theatrical ceremony of soldiers in 18th century uniforms, held at 9pm every evening at La Cabaña fortress on the other side of the harbour. Like the firing of the noon-day guns in Cape Town and Hong Kong, this canon firing tradition, which has survived colonial and political change, is well worth witnessing.

| *Daily Mail* | **Straight to the point** | 5 Dec |

Sarah Vine (Dec 5) ought to know that children whose parents spend £30,000 a year on school fees won't be walking home, as at those fees, they will be at boarding schools.

| *DTel* | **Nativity slant** | 5 Dec |

SIR - Other than using horses rather than camels to carry the kings and wise men to see Him, I am at a loss to see from the account of the Wintershall nativity play (Letters, December 5) how it provides "a different slant on Jesus" to any other such play; or was the stable on a slope?

The Times   **Good one My Lord**   9 Dec

Sir, As a guest who has enjoyed the pleasant banter during lunch at the Old Bailey, I can confirm that our learned companions earned their meal that day (letter, Dec 9). However, full judicial costumes were not on display as there were no wigs with them, only wags.

DTel   **Ending the coalition**   9 Dec

SIR - The timing of the end of the coalition would also be important to the Conservative Party's prospects at the next election (Letters, December 9) as it could give the Prime Minister the opportunity to call it at a time of his choosing, as the Fixed-term Parliaments Act 2011 allows for an early election following a vote of no confidence.

DTel   **Wheelchairs/buggies on buses**   11 Dec

SIR – On one of the buses I used in London last week, the unseated space had clear signs showing it was for use by both wheelchairs and buggies and had enough room for one of each. This reasonable provision supports the Court of Appeal decision that possession by either user is now ten tenths of the law.

The purpose of bouncers

Ramji Abinashi is mistaken when he says that bouncers in cricket are intended to hurt (letter, 8 December). They are primarily used, sparingly and within the laws, to get a batsman out by exposing any weakness in technique - such as giving a catch through an inability to keep the ball down, or failure to protect his wicket when facing subsequent deliveries.

The freak accident which brought about the demise of Phil Hughes would not have been prevented by a red card system; though cricket lovers everywhere will now expect existing laws governing intimidatory bowling to be enforced consistently and at all levels of ability.

Daily Telegraph   16 Dec

Just popping out to warm up
a little bit (P)

SIR - We live in an old farmhouse in a frost pocket where it is colder inside than out (Letters, December 15). Setting the daytime room temperature at 22C is merely a target which is never reached. A woodburner, recently fitted in one room with three walls to the outside, is having to be upgraded to cope, contrary to the manufacturer's assurances.

In summer, when it is occasionally too hot, we come inside to cool off.

Sunday Times   **Debate or disdain?**   16 Dec

 I watched the BBC's rather unedifying broadcast of Question Time from Canterbury, on which Camilla Cavendish was a panellist ("Stuck between Brand and Farage is a place no one wants to be", December 14) and do not agree with her recollection that "We women didn't get a huge amount of airtime in this battle of the big Brands." They had plenty; and certainly if you include one woman from the audience who had more than her fair share and another who shouldn't have had any. The programme needs to get back to serious debate between the panellists. Otherwise, the trend towards more audience participation will backfire with lacklustre participation by politicians for fear of showing disdain for the public, the reverse of what the programme's producers appear to be hoping for.

DTel   **Heavens above!**   17 Dec

SIR - Your correspondents do not go far enough (Letters, December 15, 16). Solar panels should be a condition of all new grants for roofs from the Heritage Lottery Fund, starting with Canterbury Cathedral ("Pennies from Heaven", BBC Two). After all, the benefits - if not the funding - are heaven-sent.

The Times   **Cuban cigars**   20 Dec

Sir, President Obama is surely looking in awe at the Cuban cigar in his hand, not just sniffing it (front page caption, Dec 20), as it looks very much like it's a Montecristo 'A', the longest size that is made with single leaves running through it and a work of art.

DTel   **Women in the Army**   20 Dec

SIR - So for all the hype, just 28 women each year are predicted to qualify for ground combat jobs in the Army (report, December 20). I am surprised it is as many.
Col J M C Watson (Retd)

Evening Standard   22 Dec

(Spending a penny)

Michael Zehse would not have paid "one new pence" for his admission to Kew (Mon), but a new "One penny" piece, as shown on the reverse of each such coin since 1971. Have a look this Christmas.

The Times   **The chief constables' dilemma**   24 Dec

Sir, The dilemma faced by the chief constables who wish to protest to the Home Secretary about spending cuts, but are being lent on by police and crime commissioners (PCCs) ("Police chiefs bullied into silence on cuts", Dec 24) is less an example about the politicisation of policing than about exercising and retaining power. Be they chief constables, PCCs, or the home secretary, the late Tony Benn's five questions to someone with power would appear to be most apposite: "What power have you got? Where did you get it from? In whose interests do you exercise it? To whom are you accountable? How can we get rid of you?"

The Oldie **Empire matters** 30 Dec

SIR: You reveal in the Old Un's diary (January issue) that Sir Richard Eyre, a speaker at the memorial service for Lady Soames, was narrowly spared embarrassment when a reference to Zimbabwe was spotted in a play set in the 1960s, when it was still Southern Rhodesia. It seems a pity that William Shawcross had no such timely encounter before giving his eulogy at the same service (also January issue), as Lady Soames's late husband, Christopher, was not "made the last Governor General of Rhodesia at the end of 1979", but the last Governor of Southern Rhodesia.

2015

| *DTel* | **Dates in 2015** | 1 Jan |

SIR - I learnt the dates of Magna Carta, Agincourt and Waterloo as twelve-fifteen, fourteen-fifteen and eighteen-fifteen, long before having to recognise them in the Armed Forces as a quarter past these hours afternoon (Letters, January 1). I expect we will hear them repeated this way many more times this year.

| *DTel* | **Car names** | 2 Jan |

SIR – Our eldest daughter called the starter car I bought her, Basil, as she said it was always faulty.

| *The Times* | **Network Rail** | 2 Jan |

Sir, Martin Morris is being as disingenuous as he claims Sir Bob Reid to be (letters, Jan 1 and 2). It is the lengths of consecutive components on the critical path of a project which fix the end date, not the other way around. If those components take longer than planned, then the end date will slip. Safety and inspections are indeed critical and must not be compromised, but the woeful impact from the failures at King's Cross was nonetheless the result of insufficient planning and inadequate risk management by Network Rail.

DTel   **Ordnance Survey**   6 Jan
for delivery drivers

SIR - Our post code shows on satnav that we live on the M4 between junctions 13 and 14; some delivery drivers only discover that we don't when they hear "You have now reached you destination", while driving along it. The house is marked clearly and by name on Ordnance Survey maps, but too few drivers are provided with this reversionary method of navigation or the training to use it. The best hope we have is for a driver who has been before, as some give up altogether.

STel   **Flying east-west**   6 Jan

SIR - Bruce Denness asks about a possible manufacturing aberration with shirt buttonholes (Letters, January 4). I recently acquired a pair of pyjamas where the jacket buttonholes all run east-west – a nuisance - and three buttons sewn onto the trouser bottoms embellish a false fly – an abomination.

Evening Standard 8 Jan

(Redundant runways)

James Page says that a new runway would never be put back to grass (Tue); but this is not necessarily the case. The once longest military runway in Europe at Greenham Common was broken up as part of the restoration of the Greenham and Cookham Commons when it was no longer needed.

DTel **Non-worshippers** 13 Jan
and the Church of England

SIR - Worshippers are believers and the Church of England congregation will not increase while the number of believers continues its inexorable decline ("Archbishops warn of urgent battle for new worshippers", January 13). Any renewal and reform needs to recognise this and accept that there are those brought up in the Church's traditions who do not worship and are not going to be converts, who nonetheless acknowledge the many benefits that Christianity has brought us and who do much good in their own ways. Making an offer to non-worshippers relevant to their lives in the 21st Century would be a start.

The Times	**The last smile**	14 Jan

Sir, Amused at being described as dour, perhaps George Churchill-Coleman's re-recorded message on his answering machine was more likely at the time to have been, "Hello, it's Smiley here" (Obituary, Jan 13). [Rather than "smiley" as published.]

Sunday Times	**Newsnight**	15 Jan
Culture section		

I suggest that Newsnight (BBC2) has three formidable female presenters, but that only two of them are excellent; Evan Davis is excellent, if not so formidable.

The Times	**Sports tattoos**	17 Jan

Sir, Kevin Pietersen will have won "the worst tattoo in sport" hands down if this latest innovation - the reverse draw - has indeed left him with a mirror image of a map of the world on his back, as pictured (Sport, page 11, Jan 17).

Sunday Times   **A question of love**   19 Jan

Of "The 36 questions that lead to love" (Focus, January 18), only 26 contained questions, while the remaining 10, including seven of the 12 in Set Three, were actually commands. Presumably those adopting this approach would have no difficulty in including "obey" in any marriage vows.

Daily Telegraph   22 Jan

Original Alice (P online)

SIR - Alice Jaspars (Letters, January 20) asks why Royal Mail has not used John Tenniel's illustrations from the original 1865 edition of *Alice in Wonderland* on its stamps to mark the 150th anniversary of publication.

Tenniel's illustrations of Alice, the Mad Hatter and the Cheshire Cat appeared in a set to commemorate the Year of the Child in 1979; the Cheshire Cat in a series of famous smiles in 1990; and Tweedledum and Tweedledee in 1993.

Perhaps for 2020, the bicentenary of Tenniel's birth, Royal Mail might consider a full series to commemorate his work.

The Times   **Of off and on**   24 Jan

Sir, Oliver Kamm says that "off of", meaning "off", is completely acceptable in speech (The Pedant, Register, Jan 24) and in a variety of dialects. But I wonder if this extends to the meaning "on" in Geordie, as comedian Ross Noble tells theatre audiences that he is always being mistaken for the Scottish television presenter Neil Oliver "off of" *Coast*.

The Times   27 Jan

In the name of God

Sir, As we remember the death of Sir Winston Churchill 50 years ago, we should not forget that Oliver Cromwell's words to the rump parliament (letter, Jan 26) were quoted in the Commons in May 1940, amid cheers, by Leo Amery. Churchill wrote in *The Gathering Storm* that "These were terrible words, coming from a colleague of many years . . . a privy counsellor of distinction"; they led to Neville Chamberlain's resignation three days later.

DTel   **Churchillian drinking**   28 Jan

SIR - I remember sharing 750ml bottles of champagne over dinner with a brother officer during the 1969 point-to-point season (Features, January 28). We also drank it out of silver tankards, with Angostura bitters and grapefruit juice added, but I don't recall it lasting for four courses, or even three – just the horrendous mess bills.

Evening Standard   **Money well spent**   30 Jan

Farnham Castle has long provided intercultural competence and awareness seminars and briefings, for which the FCO and MoD are clients. DfT should join them before they next send abroad Baroness Kramer, their minister responsible for international matters (Texts, Thu).

The Times **Turnover taxes** 30 Jan

Sir, Chris Brown identifies a revision of the tax rules as a way of dealing with minimal taxation paid by multinational corporations, suggesting that a tax on turnover could be part of it (letter, Jan 30). However, as a member of the EU, the UK may not introduce any taxes, duties or charges that could be characterised as turnover taxes. Another reason to leave the EU, or just one to add to the list for renegotiation?

The Cricketer **Cricketing knights** 1 Feb

Michael Henderson makes light of the honours system for elevating the actress Joan Collins to a damehood, for services to 'charidee' (Bouncer, Feb issue). Well she is in good company, as Sir Ian Botham was also elevated for services to charity, raising more than £12 million for causes such as research into leukaemia.

Of the other England cricketers Henderson lists, who were indeed knighted for services to cricket, Sir Pelham Warner's dubbing in 1937 preceded rather than followed the knighthood for Sir Jack Hobbs in 1953.

| *The Times* | **Fear not** | 2 Feb |

Sir, There may be less to fear than Libby Purves imagines ("We fear the Queen's demise, not Charles's rise", Feb 2). I heard a couple of years ago of an actuarial estimate that the Queen could live to be 116, in which case the Prince of Wales could well predecease her.

| *The Times* | **Mistaken motto** | 3 Feb |

Sir, I remember an edition of the US magazine *Armed Forces Journal* dedicated to their Special Forces. It had to be reissued as the cover had on it "First in, first out" (Letter, Feb 3).

| *DTel* | **White is cool** | 5 Feb |

SIR - Wearing nothing but black is not confined to the world of fashion (Letters, February 5). Seeing Andy Murray wear black for the final of the Australian Open reminded me of how the golfer Gary Player made the colour his own; a similar opportunity must be available for a modern-day tennis player, but for white.

   The player adopting all-white would stand out among the other players wearing multiples of colours and, as white reflects the heat, could be cool in both senses of the word. Even at Wimbledon, all-white would be distinctive as the other competitors always go for permitted permutations of nearly all-white.

Someone should try it. Gary Player had a huge following and became one of the greatest players in the history of golf.

The Oldie **Churchill 50 years on** 5 Feb

SIR: After watching again on television Sir Winston Churchill's funeral 50 years on, I went through all the magazines and cuttings which I had kept at the time. I was familiar with all the pictures, but two articles in particular caught my attention and, in these days of electronic access to newspaper archives, may be of interest to readers. Both were published the day after the funeral.

The first, titled "Goodbye, Dear Friend" in *The Sunday Times*, was by Field-Marshal Montgomery who was unable to join what he called the last homage due to illness and absence in South Africa. In it he tells the story of their friendship which only began in 1945 when Churchill was discarded by the nation. The second, titled "The Man I Knew" in *The Observer*, was by Lord Attlee in which he describes how they worked together and that the only thing that Churchill had against him was that he was a Socialist. These accounts, from their different angles, are well worth reading.

| *Private Eye* | **Pedantry Corner** | 5 Feb |

… Martin Smith (Pedantry Corner , Eye 1385) is not entirely correct when he says that Lady Kennedy can only be styled "Lady **Helena** Kennedy" if she is the daughter of a hereditary peer. Only as the daughter of a duke, a marquess or an earl would that be correct; as the daughter of a viscount or a baron she would be styled "The Honourable Helena Kennedy".

| *The Lady* | 6 Feb |

Once in a lifetime

Janet Price writes movingly about the diagnosis of her husband's motor neurone disease and her discovery that a GP may only see one person with MND in 30 years of practice (Letters, A Special Man, 16 January issue). The same can be said of a ruptured spleen.

My life was saved in 1971 by a surgeon who suspected the rupture and operated immediately, after my collapse *15 hours earlier* had mystified GPs and hospital doctors alike. A rupture is normally the result of a trauma, but in my case it was *the result of having an enlarged spleen* due to undiagnosed glandular fever.

There are always exceptions - I met a retired army doctor who had been faced with four ruptured spleens in 24 hours while in India.

There, most people [had] *suffered to some degree with* malaria, which *also* causes the spleen to swell and *death could even be inflicted by a sharp jab with the fingers under the ribs, leaving no trace of foul play.*

Awareness may be helpful, but GPs actually coming across a rupture will remain statistically rare.

Italics edited out.

| *The Times* | **Google pronunciation** | 8 Feb |

Sir, It is not only the pronunciation of place names that Google may need to address (letter, Feb 9). American friends staying with us returned from a shopping trip confidently announcing that they had been to *Duh-ben-ams*.

Evening Standard   **Lucy Who?**   12 Feb

Lucy Mangan may be closer to time travel than she imagines (Comment, Thurs), as the Sam Wanamaker Playhouse is not 400 years old at all. Having been constructed using 17th century plans for an indoor theatre, it opened just one year ago.

The Spectator   **Pedestrians beware**   13 Feb

I once attended a demonstration of a driverless vehicle in Denver, Colorado. It had to be stopped when the vehicle was no longer able to identify the distinction between the edge of the test track and the grass verge after a snowfall. Since then I have always been rather sceptical of trials being undertaken in places like California and now Milton Keynes in the spring (Long Life, February 14).

DTel   **God save us**   16 Feb

SIR - Having seen six-year-old Harry Westlake sing the National Anthem on breakfast television and now read the feature about him ("England mascot who sang his heart out and won the world over", February 16), I wonder if there would have been quite so much coverage if those editing the pieces recognised that he was taught the wrong words. The line is not "God save our Queen", but "God save the Queen".

STel **Indian Summers** 17 Feb

SIR - James Bishop needn't have worried too much about the lesser spotted shrimp flying in Simla in December in Channel 4's *Indian Summers* (Letters, February 15). Continuity errors in the first episode were far too distracting for that sort of thing to be noticed.

The viceroy's secretary's collar was up at the back of his neck in one shot, then down in the next from a different angle; a picture hung too low on the wall by Julie Waters' character had miraculously risen after she had taken her hands away. No one was listed in the credits for continuity, so there could be lots more spotting to be done in the weeks ahead.

The Times **No tea ceremony out there** 18 Feb

Sir, The pleasure of drinking tea has never been confined to the finest surroundings, china, or ingredients (letters, Feb 18 and 19). In his acclaimed recollection of the war in Burma, *Quartered Safe Out Here* (1992), author the late George MacDonald Fraser revealed that without a teapot the casting of the tea leaves into a gallon of water boiled in a brew-can was the crucial thing, followed by two broken match sticks to attract stray leaves. It was then scooped out with enamelled mugs, "each man adding sugar and condensed milk to taste."

DTel **Card from Father Christmas** 20 Feb

SIR - Perhaps the Christmas card Anne McWIlliam received with the greeting "...for someone I seldom see" came from Father Christmas; she just guessed it was from her husband (Letters, February 20).

The Times **The Watson Papers** 22 Feb

Sir, What exciting news that the story, *Sherlock Holmes: Discovering the Border Burghs and, by Deduction, the Brig Bazaar*, has been uncovered in an attic in Scotland - 50 years after the *Flashman Papers* were found in a Leicestershire saleroom – but how uninspiring of you to suggest that it should remain unpublished (Leading article, Feb 21). Dr Watson surely had some exciting adventures of his own to tell us.

DTel **Depressing terms** 24 Feb

SIR - Having heard the two former foreign secretaries defending their actions, may I suggest a *legal low* as a new and depressing term for contemporary usage (Letters, February 23, 24).

Sir Malcolm Rifkind and Jack Straw were later found not to have broken parliamentary rules, but see pages 196 and 197.

Country Life   25 Feb

From the mascot horse's mouth

Ellie Hughes rightly highlights the distinction between 'official' and 'unofficial' in her article about regimental mascots (*February 11*). As a young captain in 1976 I was given the dubious honour of moving a forerunner of The Queen's Royal Hussars' drum horse, called Dettingen, from its quarters in Warminster to Detmold, West Germany. Ignorant of the full significance of the horse's status, I was relieved to discover, that as an 'official' mascot, it was moved at public expense. All I eventually did was fill in a form, which I have never forgotten was a T998 - I expect it may be still in use today.

The Times   **Term-time for work and play**   2 Mar

Sir, Where I was at school in the Fifties and Sixties there were no half-terms - or long weekends instead - just eight weeks holiday between July and September; and the only school outings on offer at the end of the summer term were away matches – exams permitting (letter, Mar 2). That certainly worked too, not least as none of us going on to read engineering at university had a shortfall in maths to be made up by their engineering departments (letters, Feb 7).

The Cricketer   March

Not the only way (P)

Crispin Andrews says of his favourite cricketer, Ian Chappell *("His was the only way"*, January issue), that he "doffed his Baggy Green to no one". No doubt meant metaphorically, it could also apply on the field of play.

After making 192 at The Oval in 1975 he raised neither his cap nor bat, nor made any other acknowledgement to the crowd, which applauded him all the way back to the pavilion.

Fortunately, his is not and never has been the only way - great player that he undoubtedly was.

Evening Standard **Blunt analysis** 4 Mar

Crispin Blunt MP says that the expansion of Gatwick airport would not be easy and is wholly impractical without massive new housing and surface transport infrastructure (Tues): so with the required housing and infrastructure (including extra rail capacity (Texts, Wed)), it must be practical. No one says it would be easy, but it does not follow that the surrounding towns and communities around Gatwick would be forced to grow in unsustainable ways to accommodate tens of thousands more people to work there. If it is practical, then it can also be made sustainable and cannot be so easily ruled out.

Daily Telegraph 5 Mar

Planning a purpose-built replacement for the Houses of Parliament

SIR - Charles Holden (Letters, March 4) is right that we need a building that is really fit for purpose for our future governance to be effective.

However, by the time the case has been made and a decision delayed, then taken; the project funded, then cut; the specification agreed, altered, then finally completed and modified before occupation, it will need to be fit for the 22nd century, never mind this one.

The Times	**The profit test**	5 Mar

Sir, If everyone ate the food they had that passed the three tests of look, smell and taste (Letter, Mar 5), less food would be bought. Dates on food won't be abolished by purveyors voluntarily, as to do so would fail their own tests on cost, price and sales, used to maximise profit.

The Times	**Spending on defence**	7 Mar

Sir, Defence spending has declined at one per cent of GDP per decade in peacetime: 2 per cent now, down from 8 per cent in 1953 (Letters, Mar 7). However, this has been justified in real terms when the required budget has been met by the necessary growth in the economy. Both the budget and the percentage of GDP need to be considered together, along with the prevailing economic conditions, for reasoned analysis. It is not surprising then that the Conservatives will not commit to 2 per cent of GDP while championing a reviving economy.

The Times   **Positions of letters**   11 Mar

Sir, For letters about England's latest efforts at cricket I'm aiming for bottom bottom (letter, Mar 11).

The newspaper had moved its letters from the right page to the left, prompting a correspondent to question whether he should now be aiming for bottom-left or bottom-right.

Sunday Times   **You say**   15 Mar
Culture section

It is the continuity during the filming, not the adverts in the breaks, that spoils **Indian Summers** (C4): collars up and then down, different jacket buttons done up or undone, a picture moving position, and all between shots. But to hear "Pleased to meet you", in 1932 – I laughed out loud.

DTel   **CA? Non**   15 Mar

SIR - If indeed there is one thing that fans can be sure of in the new James Bond movie, *Spectre* - 007's nemesis will not be Mexican - then another is that Mexico is in fact a country in North not Central

America ("How Bond got into bed with Mexico to save £13m, March 14).

The Times   18 Mar

Robin's nest

Sir, I am not sure we all learnt *Home Thoughts from Abroad*, with its mention of the wise thrush (letter, Mar 18). A more likely poem for us all to have learnt might be Thomas Hood's *I Remember, I Remember*, in which the robin features. This could account for it coming top of the short list.

The Oldie   **Scarborough's fair**   18 Mar

SIR: Your *Go Away Great Britain* travel special (April issue), a guide to Britain through its festivals, contained a nostalgic feature on the resort, but omitted to mention the Scarborough Cricket Festival, which has attracted thousands of holidaymakers since 1876. Many of the world's greatest players have played there, including Fred Trueman who used to entertain the crowds by pretending to be shot while fielding, as the bangs from another enduring attraction - the unique naval warfare re-enactment using large scale models on the nearby boating lake at Peasholm Park - carried to the ground. The first English seaside resort and the last to maintain a professional orchestra, Scarborough is not short of cultural events, but there the term "festival" will always be associated with cricket first.

DTel   **Luck of the spine**   20 Mar

SIR - Medicine may not be just a lottery in this country (Letters, March 20). In the USA nearly 30 years ago, I also had a pain in the back, near the spine, as I was sent over three months from a doctor in primary care to a physiotherapist, then an orthopaedic surgeon and finally a neurosurgeon, who only had to see me walk towards him to know that I had a ruptured disc and at what level. At least I was lucky that this led to a successful, if belated, operation and no further trouble.

Independent   20 Mar

Opt out of the junk mail

Trevor Beaumont (letter, 19 March) should register with Royal Mail's Door-to-Door Opt-Out, a free service which will stop the junk mail leaflets being put through his letter box. It takes a bit of time to come into effect, but when it does his postman is as likely to lose his job for continuing to deliver the offending items as he is for not delivering them now.

A correspondent wrote the following day thanking me for the helpful advice, but had noticed on the website that the service did not include "the stacks of glossy depictions of pizzas, burgers, double-glazed windows and smug estate agents, the Parish Newsletter, invites to a glass of wine with the Residents Association, or those plastic bags from charities."

Independent   23 Mar

Yes, but what is junk mail

May I reassure Mike Lewis (letter, 21 March) that I no longer receive from Royal Mail's Newbury sorting office any of the offending items he fears will keep coming, though the Parish Newsletter arrives by another hand?

The Times   **Test cricket**   25 Mar

Sir, Mike Atherton, commentating on Sky TV as New Zealand beat South Africa in the World Cup semi-final said, if inadvertently, "There is a winner, there is a loser, as there always is in sport." This is not the case in Test cricket, where a drawn match or series can still be a thrilling and fair result. I hope that Andrew Strauss will use his position on the ICC cricket committee to ensure that cricket's sternest contest, played over two innings, is not allowed to die (Sport, Mar 24).

The Times   **Aircraft safety**   27 Mar

Sir, The simple suggestion of another member of the crew in the cockpit and video cameras fitted to passenger aircraft are stop-gap solutions (letters, Mar 27). In this age of unmanned aerial vehicles in war zones and a one-way voyage to die on Mars, it should be within our technological capabilities to override a human induced gross error in a monitored flight path of an aircraft destined to crash back on Earth. A reprioritisation of advances in air and space travel must be undertaken as a matter of urgency.

| *The Times* | **Great music** | 28 Mar |

Sir, To the ears of many, and worldwide, there has been a memorable amount of great music produced in the last century and a half (letter, Mar 28). Whether or not it was inspired by Darwinian science, most of it was not written by classical composers.

| *DTel* | **The end of the Sabbath** | 28 Mar |
| *Evening Standard* | | 30 Mar |

SIR - Could the religion of a seven-day NHS be the final nail in the coffin for prayer as a remedy?

| *Independent* | | 31 Mar |

The voters' favourite –
None of the Above

Readers will be interested to hear of a further benefit in the coming weeks from opting out of receiving junk mail through the post (letters, 19, 20, 21, 23 March).

The postman tells me that he will not be delivering leaflets to us from any of the political parties in the run-up to the General Election. Thank you, Royal Mail.

The Times	**Dem bones**	1 Apr

Sir, A competition in *The Spectator* magazine is inviting readers to suggest suitable Desert Island Discs for a well-known historical figure, living or dead. I am now left wondering whether 'Dem bones dem dry bones' sung by Fats Waller, earmarked for Richard III, is not more appropriate for William Shakespeare (letters, Mar 31, Apr 1).

DTel	**The King's Champion**	3 Apr

SIR - In 1983, I played King George IV at the Berlin Military Tattoo in a grand musical finale based on his Coronation, during which the King's Champion rode into the arena as described in the obituary of Lt Col John Dymoke (April 3); including a gauntlet being thrown to the ground and a herald crying out that whoever challenged the King's right to the crown must engage the Champion in mortal combat. No one picked up the gauntlet, but I did not get to drink wine from a gold cup in the Champion's honour, as I now know was the custom. I shall be having a word with the producer.
Col Malcolm Watson (Retd)

Private Eye	**Pedantry corner**	4 Apr

...Re the cover of Eye 1389 "How the election will work", the bubble spoken by the Queen and Alex Salmond should of course read "After the voting someone comes to me and *I ask them* to form a government".

The Times		6 Apr

East is East

Sir, Your quiz master, Olav Bjortomt, seems to be all at sea with his views on what constitutes the East (Feedback, April 4).

From the early 20th century the East started at Alexandria. From there, the Near East was where you were told that you shouldn't be wearing a white dinner jacket, as you weren't east of Suez. The Far East was where you had a white dinner jacket made to wear there and in the Middle East, as well as a lightweight black dinner jacket to wear back in the Near East.

Evening Standard   **Mansion management**   7 Apr

I am not sure whether those who work for Savills - surely one of London's, if not the world's leading estate agents - will be laughing or crying at being described in your leading article (Tues) as a "property management firm"; then, maybe both.

Evening Standard   **Yeah, yes**   8 Apr

A clue to what people mean when they say "yeah, no" (Texts, Tues) may possibly be found from the Spanish "cómo no", which as a question means "why not?", but in exclamation means "of course!", the latter especially in Latin America.

The Times   **Ed the groom**   11 Apr

Sir, I was so pleased to read that Ed Miliband was not a virgin bride (Janice Turner, Apr 11): he seems to have enough thrown at him without having to cope with questions about a change of gender.

Evening Standard   **Politics at the manor**   13 Apr

Though W Forbes-Hamilton's notion of a
Conservative and Labour government is a serious one
(Texts, Fri), I cannot help myself imagining it being
suggested by Penelope Keith in *To the Manor Born.*

The Times   **Illustrate and be published**   14 Apr

Sir, Joan Olivier is rightly proud of her letters
published in *The Times*, but wonders what to do with
them (letter, Apr 14). I have recently been
approached by the cartoonist Bill Tidy suggesting that
he illustrates some of mine for a joint-venture book. I
invite Joan and other practitioners with a "bottom
right" tendency to contact me at the sufficiently
detailed address, below, with a view to widening its
content and appeal.

DTel   **Nothing added**   14 Apr

SIR - I don't suppose that the late Richie Benaud
(Obituary, April 11) would have "felt he could add to
the picture" of Kate Winslet by describing what is so
clearly a "blue dress with a scooping neckline"
(News, April 14), even for his column in the *News of
the World.*

Drafted but not sent:

The Times   ***Lives remembered***   15 Apr

Richie Benaud

Malcolm Watson writes: *I once stood next to Richie Benaud (Obituary, Apr 11) in the urinals at Headingley. I was surprised how tall he was.*

Cricket Paper   17 Apr

Bring back Pietersen*

Well done public schoolboy Tom Harrison, Chief Executive of the ECB, for his energetic lead and decisive action. There is no arrogance on display here (letter, April 10), just reasoned argument.

*The subject of the letter above mine, but not mine above.

Daily Telegraph   18 Apr

Cool as a cucumber (P online)

SIR - Research shows that a wrapped cucumber lasts three times longer than an unwrapped one and loses less weight through evaporation.

What interests me, though, is why supermarkets sell their brandy in plastic bottles, but all other spirits in glass. It certainly doesn't last any longer in my drinks cupboard.

Country Life   22 Apr

The smoking code? (P)

I was interested to read that your cigar correspondent smokes a cigar not just with one band on, but two (*Bolivar, April 1*). English etiquette calls for the band(s) to be removed, though in these non-judgemental days purveyors are now likely to tell customers that it is optional, or a 'personal choice'. However, the second band towards the middle of the cigar needs to be removed if you want to smoke past it and thus well into the last third, as such cigars 'aged in the stick' surely warrant.

It is one thing to have been given a new type of cigar to assess and been able to enjoy the flavours 'right until the second band began to char', yet quite another to pay good money for it, wish to savour it and not have it taste like burnt paper.

If you do get to try one, I recommend letting the cigar burn for 10 minutes or so to soften the glue that holds the label to the wrapper, then undoing it at the seam before removing, at the very least, that second band to ensure full satisfaction.

Ed-This question of cigar etiquette is interesting and I am not sure that I know the answer to it. Some say that cigar bands were first created to avoid marking gentlemen's white gloves or fingers with tobacco stains. Whatever the truth, they are certainly useful brand markers and become more decorative and elaborate over the years.

DTel   **Spirits for motoring**   22 Apr

SIR - In the late Seventies in West Germany it
cost less to use duty-free vodka from the NAAFI than
screenwash in my car (Letters, April 22). I often
wondered about crème de menthe for the radiator
and cherry brandy for the brake fluid.

The Times   **Election rights**   23 Apr

Sir, Anthony Werner asks if it is time to remind
ourselves of our right to elect our leaders (letter,
Apr 23). However, our right is to elect members of
parliament and it is they who will have the
responsibility to provide workable governance in the
event of a hung parliament. Some candidates and
commentators, such as David Blunkett (letter, Apr
23), seem to be much more aware of this than others.

The Times   **James Bond from Yorkshire**   24 Apr

Sir, As a Tyke myself, I approve of David Cameron's
suggestion on the radio that the next 007 should be a
Yorkshireman, but cannot agree with his choice of
William Hague. The youthful cricketer, Joe Root,
already performing heroic deeds for England in
foreign parts (Sport, Apr 24), must have a more
realistic prospect of scoring in all areas.

DTel   **Garlic bread**   27 Apr

SIR - Bob Pinford asks why supermarket garlic bread always comes in nine slices (Letters Apr 26). Take a loaf, slice it with 10 evenly spaced cuts and discard the outer two crusts. Voilà! Nine slices ready for garlic butter to be applied and packaged for sale, no doubt all done by machine.

The Times   **Game and sports**   29 Apr

Sir, My understanding, as an occasional cigar smoker, is that sports such as hunting, shooting and fishing, being conducted outdoors, offer some of the few remaining opportunities to smoke in company without attracting disapproval.

Fortunately, at Lord's, some seating is still reserved in the pavilion so that I can smoke while watching my favourite game (letter, Apr 29).

The Times   **Better Renting for Britain**   1 May

Sir, "Build to rent" is certainly a different business model (letter, May 1). Didn't any of the 41 signatories realise that they meant "build to let" or "build for rent"?

Sunday Times   7 Jun
Culture section

(Indian Summers 2)

I was astonished to hear "going forward" uttered during the last episode - and even more so to hear voiced over the credits that indeed they were going to have another series next year.

DTel   **Smarter cars**   5 May

SIR - In case anyone is still wondering about changing the digital display of speed in cars (Letters, May 2), my 2004 Toyota Yaris changes from "MPH" to "km/hr" at the touch of the Mode button just below the display. Surely a new car could be expected to change the speed mode and time as it crosses the Channel, just as they do on a smart mobile phone?

Sunday Times   **Winging it**   5 May

Whatever Jeremy Clarkson thinks Village People did for the navy, Top Gun didn't do it for the air force, as the film was about naval aviators (News Review, May 4).

Private Eye   **Pedantry Corner**   5 May

….Back in Wisden, Alex Murray (letter, Eye 1391) will find that Richie Benaud played in Test (not test) matches and series, whether they were won or lost. I feel quite relieved to get that off my chest.

Daily Telegraph   9 May

The election was clinched by the twin factors of Labour's inadequacies and a justified fear of the SNP dictating policy*(P)

SIR - When John Major lost the election in 1997, he went to The Oval in the afternoon to watch Surrey.

I hope cricket-loving Ed Balls will find equal solace in supporting Yorkshire at Headingley, starting tomorrow, and England when they play there later this month.

*One of 29 letters published under the only banner on the Saturday after the general election.

The Times **So much Balls** 10 May

Sir, Your leading article (May 9) says that "Ed Balls, the shadow chancellor, fell to a swing from Labour to the Conservatives that stunned pollsters and was repeated across much of England", but Balls had just a 2.3% or 1,101 majority in 2010. What was surprising was that the victor, Conservative candidate Andrea Jenkyns, seemed so stunned by the result.

The Times **Kevin Pietersen** 13 May

Sir, Did BBC's *Newsnight* really need to field their "Croquet Correspondent" to explain that Kevin Pietersen (letters, May 13) still needed to get through some hoops before he is recalled to play cricket for England again?

The Times 15 May

Shift to the left

Sir, Further to the letter "Vote for the right" (May 11), I have started to read the letters page from the bottom left, with "Corrections and clarifications".

These admissions of fallibility are both welcome and informative.

Independent   19 May

The jobs MPs are elected to do

It is disingenuous of J H Moffatt (letter, May 12) to say that people who voted for smaller parties get no representation at all.

Everyone who voted, for whichever party, as well as those who did not vote, is represented by the person who got the most votes in their constituency: their local MP. MPs of all political persuasions are acutely aware of their responsibilities in this respect, but it seems that some of the electorate are not.

DTel   **Commitment in**   19 May
                the Church of England

SIR - David Bamford bemoans his need for a "Permission to Officiate" (Letters, May 19). However, it is not just "committed qualified personnel", but regular worshippers that the Church of England lacks in its parishes. It seems entirely reasonable that a Parochial Church Council should vouch to its bishop that a lay reader over 70 years of age has its blessing to continue to officiate, assuming that it doesn't want its congregation to decline any further, by either agreeing, or not, to his or her continuance.

The Spectator   **Use of the vernacular**   25 May

Sir, In his support for the rebuilding of the Euston Arch (Restoration drama, May 23), William Cook describes Euston as London's most miserable train station. A more joyful restoration might be the return of "railway" station to the nation's vernacular.

The Times   **Monty and foreign leaders**   26 May

Sir, During his talk to my school in 1963, Field Marshall Montgomery (letter, May 26) told us that the Chancellor of West Germany, Dr Adenauer, needed a large dose of weed killer. I expect he would have found the pork belly served at Chequers to the President of the European Commission, Jean-Claude Juncker, to be rather unadventurous ("Britons won't accept Europe status quo, PM tells Juncker", May 26).

Evening Standard   29 May

First-class rail travel is necessary

Kristen de Keyser says "commuting is a nasty necessity for most – it is not a luxury to be enjoyed in first class". Many trains coming from further afield have more than half first-class carriages. They are full of commuters who are clearly prepared to pay a considerable premium to make their equally necessary but longer journeys more agreeable.

DTel   **Motorway signs**   1 Jun

SIR - A sign above a 50mph stretch on the M1 says "Drive carefully through the roadworks". Fortunately, the cones guide vehicles away from them.

DTel   **More signs**   2 Jun

SIR – My favourite sign, by a car park, is "Short stay toilets".
Jane Watson

| *The Spectator* | **Success in Sierra Leone** | 2 Jun |

Sir: Colin Freeman is mistaken in his thought-provoking article ('How to defeat a caliphate', 30 May) in saying that peace was not restored in Sierra Leone until 2000 "when Tony Blair dispatched British paratroopers to run the RUF out of town"; they were there for an operation to evacuate non-combatants.

It was on the initiative of Brigadier David Richards, the commander on the ground, that they were used so decisively, for which he was awarded the DSO. He went on to be head of the army and Chief of the Defence Staff, 2010-2013.

Colonel (retired) J M C Watson

| *Sunday Times* | 7 Jun |
| *Culture section* | |

(You Say – short changed)

Bring back the You Say panel on Saturday - immediately!

They didn't, but published this, along with a similar comment, on Friday's You Say panel.

Daily Telegraph   8 Jun

Straightforward slip-up

SIR - Nick Perry has misread the sign for a slippery road (Letters, June 6). The image of tyre-tracks is indicative of the vehicle having done a 180 degree spin to the left and is now facing backwards.

Adding a pair of headlights and a driver on the left might have made this clearer.

The Times   **Views for** all   8 Jun

Sir, The arguments for not spending money on tunnelling to avoid unsightly routes through our scenic heritage (letters, June 6 & 8) are the best possible ripostes to the apocryphal quip: "What a lovely view", "Yes, is there one for the other ranks?"

DTel   **Cabinet resignations**   8 Jun

SIR - When David Cameron does not secure the major reforms from Brussels he expects and recommends leaving the EU, will those cabinet ministers wishing to stay in it be expected to resign?

Evening Standard   9 Jun

Airport decision is still some way off (P)

You are right to say that "all the relevant factors, including the environmental ones, have been taken into account" in the Davies report. However, it is the weighting that each factor has been given that will be scrutinised by both ministers and the public, *particularly if any change in weighting could lead to a change in recommendations**. If so, getting on with it may still be some way off.

J M C Watson

*Edited out.

Evening Standard   **The other JD**   10 Jun

If teenage pupils at private schools spend weekends working at JD Sports stores rather than going on expensive gap years (News, Wed), what are they going to do for the rest of the week? They could do worse than work in pubs for the other JD, Wetherspoon, but in many cases they would be best

advised to forego the gap year and start their
university courses.

Isle of Wight County Press	**Services before jobs**	12 Jun

You report on your front page (June 12) that, come
September, Havenstreet will be left without a single
bus and that Niton and Whitwell will find themselves
with a service almost cut in half. And yet, faced
with £1 million cuts the Southern Vectis general
manager, Matt Kitchen, said that the service cuts
would not result in any job losses.

Southern Vectis is in business to provide bus
services, not jobs. They must be forced to think again.

The Times	**Working after lunch**	14 Jun

Sir, Hugo Rifkind bets that most famous literary
boozers actually stayed dry until the writing was over
("Last orders for the lunchtime booze generation",
June 13). The late Keith Waterhouse, a heavy
drinker, often claimed that God had blessed him with
the gift of the delayed hangover, one that kicked in
only when he had done his day's work. Lunch was
his only hobby, leading to his authoritative and witty
manual, *The Theory and Practice of Lunch* (1986), which
even today could be a good antidote to Rifkind's *Ibiza
Uncovered*.

Country Life   17 Jun

A stamp a day keeps
the doctor away (P)

I am proud to be a third-generation stamp
collector and have recently consolidated six
collections, while at the same time
expanding the Great Britain (GB) and
Commonwealth content and creating a
second GB collection for any of the next
generation who might take an interest -
sadly, none does. However, the interesting
pointer uncovered by Anna Tyzak
(*'Philately will get you everywhere', June 3*)
'that stamp collectors live, on average, an
extra seven years' may help attract their
attention.

Two years ago, I arranged for my father a
subscription to *Stamp Magazine*, which he
still enjoys today at the age of 95, having
outlived all his non-stamp-collecting
contemporaries. The pleasure we get from
seeing such iconic items as a recently
acquired GB £1 PUC (illustrated) mounted
in the collection, along with many lower

cost space-fillers, could well be helping him on the final stretch to 100 and, I hope, my own longevity.

J. M. C. Watson, Berkshire

Private Eye **Pedantry Corner** 17 Jun

Re: "Should Test Match cricket be taken away from England?" (Daily Qatarigraph, Eye 1394), MCC would not have accused the Qataris of racism and declined their offer of hosting the forthcoming Ashes series in the Sahara desert, but passed on the offer to the ECB (England and Wales Cricket Board). England has not toured abroad under MCC colours since 1997.
PS. It's Lord's not Lords' ("An England Cricket Team", same Eye). An Apology?

Er…whoops….. Thanks very much for this. All points noted.

Ed

DTel **Serving on** 18 Jun

SIR - Not all of those completing their National Service "couldn't wait to get back into Civvy Street" (Letters, June 17) - some became Regulars and went on to have fulfilling careers, which they might not otherwise have considered.

STel **Labour leadership elections** 18 Jun

SIR - I discovered recently that for a one-off payment of £3 you can become a registered supporter of the Labour Party and have a vote for both the leader and deputy leader. Now that the short-lists have closed, this represents an incredible opportunity to vote for the team most likely to lose to the Conservatives at the next general election; and again I imagine for the leader, if there is a vote of no confidence as 2020 approaches. The investment can be made online.

Evening Standard **Long-range commuting** 19 Jun

Adam Maxsted (Texts, Wed) should be aware that the times when "peak rate" train fares to London apply relate to when they arrive there, not when they set off. The farther away you live and the slower the train, the earlier you must get on.

Cricket Paper **Positive moves all round** 21 Jun

One of the best things about England's performances so far this summer has been the absence of players scratching for 'positives' in front of the camera - that itself is a positive and long may it continue.

The Times **Scores to live for** 24 Jun

Sir, In bringing eight magnificent classical musical compositions to the cinema screen and to audiences of all ages, Walt Disney's *Fantasia* (1940) is surely unsurpassed (letters, June 23 and 24), except by later versions? The artistically-choreographed animations are enchanting.

DTel **Manners and work** 25 Jun

SIR - I was pleased to read that staff are still managing to leave their offices to have lunch ("Why good manners can cost companies dear", June 25). However, it is not so much excessive politeness that prevents them being challenged on a late return to the office or a fraudulent expenses claim - and clients over late payments - as a lack of moral courage and leadership. Finding such a regime on his BBC TV show *Troubleshooter*, the late Sir John Harvey-Jones would have asked "Who's in charge here?", before politely and with good humour pointing out the errors of their ways.

DTel   **Standing out with the bat**   30 Jun

SIR - Chris Yates is right that hundreds stand out now that the cricket scoreboards are correctly aligned (Letters, June 30), though ironically in Sussex's first innings of 601 for 6 declared it is the batsman's score of 19 which stands out below the other four batsmen who, most unusually, all scored hundreds (Sport, June 30).

The Times   **Junk mail**   30 Jun

Sir, You report that households wanting to stop unaddressed junk mail must join two separate schemes by post - one run by Royal Mail and one by the Direct Marketing Association - and that less than one in 50 of them is signed up ("Junk mail opt-out scheme quietly dropped", June 30). In fact, for those in rural locations at least, you need only join Royal Mail's Door-to-Door Opt-Out free service. It has been well worth the six week wait for it to take effect and since then it has only faltered, inadvertently, with a temporary postman on the route.

Cigar Aficionado   July/August issue

(Smoking cigars in Cuba)

Dear Marvin,

I was interested to read in the article "$100 in Cuban Cigars, What It Buys" in your April issue, the exhortation that travellers in Cuba should be so wary of buying cigars outside the proper channels. *While this is true if you wish to take them out of the country, as proof of purchase is now required,* You can smoke at much less cost when there if you are prepared to be more adventurous. During 16 visits I made as the non-resident British defence attaché from 1997 to 2000, a box of 25 Cohiba Espendidos on the street dropped from $50 to $25. However, the number of good ones per box probably dropped from 18 to 11, but at those prices if you don't like what you have lit, you light another one.

By all means buy from people offering deep discounts, if it is not illegal, but only from those who will take you to their apartment to choose them, as you will then be able to find them again if you are indeed truly disappointed. On one occasion I got back to Mexico with a box reminiscent of cow dung. I wonder if I am the only person to have taken a box of cigars back to Cuba and got a refund?!

Text above in italics edited out.

Malcolm Watson
Colonel (ret.) Defence Attaché
British Berkshire (sic), United Kingdom

Editors' response: You are a more adventurous cigar smoker than we are, and the Cohibas one buys on the streets of Havana are not likely to be genuine Cohibas. We stand by our advice to avoid buying cigars on the street and stick to the many fine shops in Cuba.

Sunday Times   5 Jul

Justifying aid

FCO officials will undoubtedly find that the £350m of foreign aid spent by their department on schemes including finding mates for tropical fish and teaching Shakespeare to Ecuadoreans provide value for money, but are these schemes justified under strict criteria for foreign aid spending? If they are, the criteria need tightening up.

Sunday Times   5 Jul
Sport section

(Sport letters - online)

One of the best things about England's performances at cricket so far this summer has been the absence of players scratching for 'positives' when in front of the microphone. That itself is a positive, but I suspect it may not last until September.

Evening Standard   **Night flights in daylight**   6 Jul

Of all your correspondents' comments so far, for and against a third runway at Heathrow [Letters, July 2,3], the one from the Chair of the Heathrow Association for the Control of Aircraft Noise (HACAN) that the most dramatic challenge to the runway being built is "a ban on night flights from 11am to 6pm" (sic) certainly seems the least telling.

Daily Telegraph   8 Jul

British beer lovers always go for the large glass (P)

SIR - Your leading article (July 6) says that Jane Peyton, the Beer Academy's Sommelier of the Year, is wrong about pairing beer and food. She is also wrong to urge the serving of beer in champagne flutes and brandy glasses.

Glass sizes are in general inversely proportional to the drink's strength. Small glasses of beer need constant topping up. However, champagne in a tankard has long been acceptable.

On 29 June, the 160th anniversary of the first ever edition of The Daily Telegraph, *some changes were made which included printing in bold the letters illustrated by a picture each day.*

The Times	**Jackets, ties and MCC**	18 Jul

Sir, Not only would the W G Grace lookalike have been wearing a blazer and the moustachioed MCC member a jacket with their ties (Cartoon, July 18), they would of course have been at Lord's, not Lords - another place altogether.

DTel	**Right enough**	20 Jul

SIR - Unlike Raymond Lewis (Letters, July 20), I find that if I don't reply to "Y'alright then?" silence ensues, especially on the telephone. Depending on how I am feeling, I have adopted as answers: "Right enough, thanks" or "Would you like five minutes or the full half-hour?"

The Times	**Whose holiday is it?**	22 Jul

Sir, There would appear to be as many different types of family holiday these days as there are different types of family: for boarding school children, school holidays should be family holidays anyway (letters, July 21, 22).   For children whose parents are separated, for whatever reason, they might enjoy two family holidays - but then, they might not. This modern-day dilemma seems to me to be more about the parents than the children.

Sunday Times   **Celebrity MasterChef**   24 Jul
Culture Section

Final Week on **Celebrity MasterChef** should be renamed Sorry About The Delay Week.

The Spectator   **Votes for a dream team**   24 Jul

Sir: Toby Young, in his spirited defence of the 'Tories for Corbyn' campaign ('Why I was right to vote for Jeremy Corbin', 25 July), omits to mention that for £3 a registered supporter also gets to vote on the deputy leadership of Labour Party. The chance to choose one from Angela Eagle, Stella Creasy, Caroline Flint, Ben Bradshaw, Tom Watson (no relation) to form a dream team with Corbyn must surely entice thousands, not hundreds, of Tories to register online. Also, if Labour ditches its leader as 2020 approaches, it can hardly deny registered supporters the opportunity to vote for a new leader once more. This campaign is indeed an effective political weapon and offers exceptional value for money.

Evening Standard **Airport noise** 26 Jul

Comments on the Airport Commission's approach to noise are going to increase (Prof Eccles, Fri). In assessing them, it is important to understand that an increase of 3 decibels doubles the noise, e.g. from 52 to 55 dBs. Charts illustrating affected areas aimed at allaying fears should be interpreted accordingly.

The Times 28 Jul

Attlee revisited

Sir, The oft misquoted description of Clement Attlee as "a quiet man with much to be quiet about" ("Taking a break from Number 10", July 27) is commonly attributed to Winston Churchill. However, the real quote, "a modest little man with plenty to be modest about", was actually coined by the left-wing journalist Claud Cockburn. I expect there are few that hold such views now.

The Times **The largest parish church** 1 Aug

Sir, Alan Gillham is right that St Nicholas in Great
Yarmouth is only said to be the largest parish church
in England (letter, Aug 1). St Botolph's in Boston,
Lincolnshire is the widest, the tallest to roof, and also
one of the largest by floor area, though that title is
held by the Holy Trinity in Hull.

The Times **Not yet stumped** 4 Aug

Sir, Any perceived north-south divide created by the
England and Wales Cricket Board for this summer's
Test match venues will be closed when the
Australians return in 2019, with Test matches once
again being staged at Old Trafford and Headingley
(letter, Aug 4). In any case, three of the five One-Day
Internationals against Australia next month are at Old
Trafford (2) and Headingley, which, weather
permitting, should prove far more beneficial for all
concerned than the blank days suffered so far at
Cardiff, at Lord's and now two at Edgbaston.

The Times **Labour's dream team** 8 Aug

Sir, Your leading article ("Political Parasites", Aug 8)
omits to mention that for £3 a registered supporter
can also vote for the deputy leadership of the Labour
party. This unrivalled opportunity to vote for the

dream team to keep the party out of office for the foreseeable future seems to offer exceptional value for money.

DTel   **One woman's Falls**   8 Aug

SIR - The 360-degree panoramic photograph of the Iguassu Falls (World News, August 8) is indeed breathtaking and bears out in no uncertain terms Eleanor Roosevelt's famous observation that it "makes Niagara Falls look like a kitchen faucet."

The Times   **Blazers**   10 Aug

Sir, I have a boater on which I have a cricket club hatband (letter, Aug 10). Ironically, the dark blue blazer I have worn it with is referred to in some circles as a boating jacket.

Evening Standard   12 Aug

We must resolve the Tube dispute

It is disingenuous of your correspondents [Letters, Tuesday] to claim that Tube drivers' rosters, fatigue and work/life balance are nothing to do with money: of course they are. Improvements to any of them will involve trade-offs for the same money, or more money without any trade-offs. Negotiators of both sides know this only too well.

The Times	**Airport noise levels**	14 Aug

Sir, I trust that David Moylan, aviation adviser to the Mayor of London (letter, Aug 14), includes in his brief the use of the decibel (dB) scale: an increase of 3dBs doubles the noise level. For example, those living in a 52dB envelope will hear their noise level double if the 55dB zone expands to include them.

As one of the Airports Commission's measures to limit the impacts on those living nearby is a legally binding 'noise envelope' putting firm limits on the level of noise created by the airport, graphics illustrating affected areas aimed at allaying fears should be interpreted accordingly.

The Times	**Passing the pot**	17 Aug

Sir, The dilemma, of whether or not a cohort of confused pot-head pensioners should be policed vigorously, or even at all (leading article, Aug 17), seems ripe for the approach trialled by Leicestershire police in respect of burglaries: follow-up action could be limited to those remembering that they lived at odd-numbered homes.

DTel   **Air conditioning on trains**   19 Aug

SIR - Adrian Quine writes that today's rolling stock has working air-conditioning ("A state-owned railway would be a costly mistake", August 19). I suggest that he has been lucky enough either to find it working when it needed to, or to have travelled when it didn't.

DTel   **To be PC or not be PC?**   24 Aug

SIR - It would be a pity if Jeremy Corbyn were to refuse to become a privy counsellor (News, August 22) and forego the possibility, one day, of attending Her Majesty in Council – at least he speaks the Queen's English.

Evening Standard   25 Aug

(Heads down in e-papers)

Gary Bevan should not have been surprised to see people commuting on a riverbus sunk deep into their mobiles [Letters, August 21]. In days gone by their heads would have been buried in newspapers and, being familiar with the view, they would not have been admiring it. Nowadays e-papers, including the free version of this one, can be read on mobiles and the pages turned at the touch of the screen without even the need to look up.

The Times	**Honours for deputies**	30 Aug

Sir, Janice Turner questions the medal given in the dissolution honours list to the gardener at 10 Downing Street for doing his job (Opinion, Aug 29), but does not comment on the number honoured whose job was that of a deputy. The under-gardener must be disappointed in being overlooked.

The Times	**Smart girls**	31 Aug

Sir, I can't somehow see the handing in of smartphones before bed by Year 9 pupils at Heathfield School in Ascot being effective ("Pupils should use mobiles in class, say private heads", Aug 31). Smart girls at this illustrious school will have one phone to hand in and one to take to bed.

DTel　　　**Gen Lord Richards and the NSC**　　1 Sep

SIR - Using Charles Moore's words (Notebook, Aug 31), "leaving aside" whether the accounts of debates between General Lord Richards and the prime minister derive chiefly from meetings of the National Security Council, their very limited content was cleared by the Cabinet Office for inclusion in his autobiography *Taking Command*, published last October and therefore already in the public domain.

The Times　　　**The Three C's**　　　　4 Sep

Sir, Further to the emergence of the "chilcot" and the "corbyn" as possible new entries into the English language (letters, Sept 1, 4), let us not forget the "clegg": a perceived benefit in the name of democracy, unrealised through lack of support from those eligible to vote for it.

The Lady　　　**Knowing the ways to San José**　　8 Sep

The Globetrotter (4 September issue) revealed British Airways' new service from Gatwick (GAT) to San José (SJO) in exotic Costa Rica, starting on May 4 2016. BA is also starting a new service that same day to San José (SJC) in California's Silicon Valley, but from Heathrow (LHR). Readers wanting to go to either San José should take extra care with the 3-letter airport codes (shown in brackets) when making a booking as, although the departure airports are only 45 miles apart, there are 3000 miles between the two destinations – a potentially expensive booking error to make.

Independent   **The place of civil servants**   9 Sep

Former senior civil servant, Roger Morgan, is possibly getting rather above himself in claiming that he has piloted several Bills through Parliament (Letters, IoS, 6 September). Ministers pilot Bills through both Houses of Parliament, though with the undoubted support, expertise and advice of civil servants. To have said, modestly, that he had helped pilot those Bills through Parliament would have been accurate.

The Times   **Just Visiting**   9 Sep

Sir, Tom Whipple ("How to beat, bankrupt and hang your friends", Times2, Sept 9) gives the impression that in Monopoly you are in jail when you land naturally on the square; but you're not, you're "Just Visiting".

The Times   **The first day at boarding school**   11 Sep

Sir, At two years older than Dr Canaway (letter, Sept 11), I also remember my first day at boarding school, aged eight. I sat in the back of the car as my mother drove me to the railway station, so as not to appear feeble. I signed my first letter home the following Sunday "Love from, Watson", to the amusement of both the school and home. I have never looked back on the succeeding 10 years with anything but pride. The vast majority who have attended boarding schools throughout the land remain unharmed by the experience.

Sunday Telegraph   13 Sep

BBC should not mess with a classic (P)

SIR - *With the BBC's adaptation of Lady Chatterley's Lover criticised this week as being profoundly unfaithful, perhaps*

We shouldn't expect too much from the BBC costume department.

The picture of Sir Clifford Chatterley in uniform at his wedding (report, September

6) showed him wearing a firearm in church. I don't think so.
Col J M C Watson (retd)

Italics edited out; with the letter above mine referring to "profoundly unfaithful".

DTel **Poisoned chalice?** 14 Sep

SIR - Former Labour home secretary, Charles Clarke, said on Radio 4's *Today* programme that he was aghast at Jeremy Corbyn appointing his leadership campaign manager, John McDonnell as shadow chancellor, but he may not last the course. In 1990, former prime minister, John Major, appointed his leadership campaign manager, Norman Lamont as chancellor, who then technically resigned after being offered a demotion in 1993. Ironically, it was Kenneth Clarke who then moved from home secretary to become chancellor.

STimes **BBC funding** 14 Sep

Dominic Lawson may well be right that the BBC is a contentious political issue in itself, but he is wrong to say that it is financed by what amounts to a poll tax (Comment, September 13). A poll tax is a single flat-rate-tax-per-capita on every adult family member in a household, a single rate for the TV licence covers the whole family.

The Times	**Brian Close**	16 Sep

Sir, Brian Close's penchant for cigarettes (Obituary, Sept 15) - two million in his lifetime - must have brought a new meaning to the challenge of 1000 before the end of May; one he met every year of his first-class cricket career.

Cricket Paper	**Bad light**	16 Sep

Wednesday saw the players leaving the field for bad light at the Ageas Bowl with the floodlights on and some of them wearing dark glasses. What on earth was going on?

Private Eye	**Inns – caught out**	18 Sep

Sir, Re: "Nooks and Corners" (p21, Eye 1401), you refer to Middle and Inner Temple as one of the London Inns of Court. They should, of course, have appeared in the piece as either Middle and Inner Temples, or Middle Temple and Inner Temple. Not even a gray area really.

The Times   **"Man's Hour"**   20 Sep

Sir, At last, the antidote to Radio 4's "Woman's Hour": Radio X, a radio station aimed exclusively at men ("I couldn't give a XXXX for Radio Banter", Sept 19). Why has it taken so long?

The Times   **Creative pleading**   21 Sep

Sir, It would be surprising if the signatories from the English Association (letter, Sept 21) weren't aware of the finding published in your sister paper (Sunday Times, Sept 20) that those with degrees in creative writing have the second worst job prospects, below animal science and one above sociology.

   Their call for an urgent review of the decision by Ofqual and the Department for Education to discontinue creative writing as an AS and A-level subject after 2018 looks like creative pleading.

The Times   **Love a mallard**   22 Sep

Sir, As seems to be the current practice, I will willingly pay £3 to vote for the duck (letter, Sept 23).

More than 2,150 people signed an online petition to reinstate the mallard in the design of the statue the commissioned by the Gresley Society of the great railway engineer Sir Nigel Gresley.

SIR, The last time Britain was invaded was not 1066 (Letter, September 23), but February 1797 when 1,400 members of the French Légion Noire landed on the Pencaer Peninsula just outside Fishguard.

Though it came to nothing, panic spread all over Britain when news of the invasion broke. People demanded their money from the banks - given out then in gold and silver coins - and set about burying it in their gardens where, they felt, it would be safe from French hands.

The Bank of England almost ran out of money and had no option but to issue promissory notes to the value of £1 and £2, paper money that has stayed with us ever since.

Sir: Toby Young says in his first Editor's Letter in *Spectator Life* (Autumn 2015) that he wants to give it a more irreverent tone. However, there is nothing yet - as he suggests there is in Meirion Jones's profile of Alan Yentob - to compare with Harry Cole's take on Theresa May (Winter 2014): 'She is boring. A technocrat. She is Philip Hammond with a fanny.' What does appear to be irreverent though, at least to this reader, is a not indiscernible reduction in font size. I look forward to an increase in both.

The Times   **The lady almoner**   28 Sep

Sir, The sting in the TV episode for Tony Hancock
(letter, Sept 28) and Sid James was that the bills for
their four-week stays in the local hospital were 50
guineas each. The lady almoner told them that they
"were both out of benefits. Your cards haven't been
stamped for over three months." The missing
payments of 11s/3d a week had been spent on three
months holidaying abroad.

DTel   **The emissions saga**   29 Sep

SIR - In the light of the emissions saga, will car
speedometers need to be recalibrated by
manufacturers to show the actual speed of travel,
rather than allowing an increment to help us keep
below speed limits?

STel   **Decimal coinage**   1 Oct

SIR - Robert Smith asks if the pricing of all goods to
the nearest five pence signals the end of the one pence
denomination (Letter, September 27). However, there
is no such denomination: the coin, which came in
with decimalization in 1971, shows "One Penny" on
the reverse.

DTel **Common ground** 6 Oct

SIR - How unfortunate for David Cameron - of all people - to be heard to emphasise on television news the Conservative Party's belief in *common* ground rather than common *ground*.

DTel **Scoff** 7 Oct

SIR - Pot Noodles and beans on toast were never traditional student specialities, but convenience foods ("Pot Noodles? Students prefer superfoods", October 7). Those living alone - men especially - will wish to minimise the washing-up by simply adding water or heating things. No cookbook, however attractively produced, is going to change this basic truth.

Evening Standard **Family firms** 7 Oct

Hamish McRea ended his article about the VW scandal and family firms [Sept 28] with some incorrect information about inheritance tax (IHT). The "special inheritance provisions for passing on a farm" also apply to all non-quoted family businesses (including those on AIM), providing that the business is not engaged in property or investments and the shares have been held for two years. So a family owned manufacturing business can have the same

IHT relief as a farm in this country as well as in Germany.

The Times   8 Oct

Finnegan's puzzle*

Sir, If, as Ed Goodall suggests (letter, Oct 8), James Joyce had been urging his fellow countrymen to wake up, then make no mistake, it was a comma that was missing: *Finnegans, Wake.*

* *My suggestion was* **The Dublin comma**.

Sunday Times   **Downton Abbey – again**   9 Oct
Culture section

Downton Abbey's rather dim, but likeable, Spratt could have been handling a stamp to mark the British Empire Exhibition dated 1925, but he was trying to position it in the place for the 1924 version in a printed album that hadn't yet been produced.

DTel **Standards** 11 Oct

SIR - Dr Francis can be assured that there are still some pockets of resistance in this country to the widespread lowering of standards he has observed during his visit from New Zealand (Letter, Oct 10).

They operate overtly in some of our national institutions, business communities, charitable organisations and the Armed Forces, to name but a few, where pride in appearance at work, in public and attending social events still counts.

The emergence of Jeremy Corbyn as the latest standard-bearer for non-conformity can only stiffen their resolve to encourage a return to a country where respect and tolerance are once more the norm.

The Times **Lancaster, bomber** 12 Oct

Sir, About his future, Stuart Lancaster says that "there are a lot of things to consider", but watching how the more successful sides do during the rest of the rugby World Cup doesn't appear to be one of them ("We'd have been better off going down the pub, says Vunipola", Sport, Oct 12). I do hope the players don't adopt the same approach - that is if they wish to improve and be picked again.

The Times	**Mispronunciation**	13 Oct

Sir, Ironically, one of the most frequently mispronounced words is pronunciation - not "pronounce-iation" - an error often not acknowledged until seen in writing (letters, Oct 13).

STel	**British museum steps**	13 Oct

SIR - Last weekend, I went to the British Museum to be greeted by the notices "Do not sit on the steps" and "Emergency escape" in front of the columns of the monumental South entrance, with visitors sitting on the steps right next to the notices. The Museum staff said trying to get the visitors not to sit there was as fruitful as moving the pigeons on. Both groups would undoubtedly move as quick as a flash if an emergency arose; no wonder so little notice is taken of such unnecessary strictures.

Submitted with photographic evidence.

Daily Telegraph   16 Oct

Corbyn clapping

SIR - Jeremy Corbyn is not clapping himself, he is clapping his supporters clapping him.

This trend for returning the compliment is also seen in teams clapping their fans during laps of honour at sporting venues and by contestants on television clapping appreciative audiences.

At least he has not been seen patting himself on the head yet, like some sports personalities.

A letter appeared in The Times *on the virtues of Coca-Cola as an agent for clearing choking.*

The Times   **Choking on Coca-Cola**   18 Oct

Sir, My late mother-in-law's guests nearly choked when, after she had stayed with us in Mexico, she offered them a drink of rum and Coca-Cola (letters, Oct 17). But they were pleasantly surprised to learn that, with the addition of fresh lime juice, they were enjoying a *Cuba Libre*.

The Times   **Heritage and power**   20 Oct

Sir, It is all very well for Loyd Grossman and his co-signatories to champion repairing and restoring the Grade I listed centrepiece of the Westminster world heritage site to its true glory and drive a resurgence in many craft and traditional building skills, but the emerging skills most required to make it fit to remain the seat of governance for the foreseeable future involve the addition and security of systems to encompass and enhance the use of cyberspace, not least to display the time on the tower (letters, Oct 20).

More farsighted would be to find new uses for the preserved site and embed these essential requirements in a new site, purpose-built using British expertise through seriously vetted employees, unless of course we would prefer China to invest in this sort of power as well as nuclear.

| *Evening Standard* | **"Shims"** | 21 Oct |

If low-alcohol cocktails known as "shims" are made using ingredients lower than 20 percent ABV, then Rachael Sigee is mistaken in saying that classic Pimm's is one of them [London Life, Tue]. Pimm's used for mixing with lemonade or ginger ale is 25 percent ABV.

| *DTel* | **Only a spoon** | 23 Oct |

SIR - Kevin Platt says that you only need a fork to eat most dishes in the canteen (Letters, October 23). In the field you only need a spoon, which also measures and stirs sugar, tea and coffee, and acts as a knife for

spreading on bread or biscuits.
Col J.M.C.Watson (retd)

The Times **That iconic photograph** 29 Oct

Sir, Mike Atherton has mentioned all the interesting
features about the iconic photograph of the final
wicket of the 1968 Ashes series at The Oval (Sport,
Oct 29), except perhaps one. It was the only Test
match in which those two swashbuckling batsmen
Ted Dexter and Colin Milburn played together.

STel ***Spectre*** 29 Oct

SIR: As with *Skyfall* (Letters, 11 Nov 12*), the credits
after *Spectre* make wonderful reading. Females are in
the ascendency among the draughtspersons, the
wireman is a man, but the drapesmaster is now a
woman.

*See The Wit and Wisdom of an Ordinary Subject.

Evening Standard **Bridge in the sky** 30 Oct

What a strange notion that the Garden Bridge will be
a fantastic addition to London's skyline [letter, Tues].
You will have to be below it, even on the river, for
such a background: just further pie in the sky for this

project.

DTel **New passport** 3 Nov

SIR - You report (*telegraph.co.uk*) that a new British passport has been launched with extra security features, including a perforated version of the holder's passport number, which will cause the paper to rip if tampered with. However, on checking my passport renewed only six weeks ago, I see that this feature is already incorporated in the current version. It is reassuring to find that such measures are not just added every five years to ensure passport security is as up to date as possible ("New passports boast culture and security", November 3).

The Times **Downton unhinged** 6 Nov

Sir, One doesn't need to have been collecting stamps in the first half of the 20th century (letter, Nov 6) to realise that the likeable Spratt in *Downton Abbey* was trying to put the 1925 commemorative issue into a printed album that hadn't yet been published.

The Spectator **Cinco de Mayo** 7 Nov

Sir: Taki asks, from the USA, what the hell Cinco de Mayo is (High Life, 31 October): "A dance step, a rumba band?" The Fifth of May is the date observed to commemorate the Mexican army's unlikely victory over French forces at the Battle of Puebla on that day in 1862, during the Franco-Mexican War (1861-1867). In this year of Mexico in the UK (and UK in Mexico), when we have remembered the 600th and 200th anniversaries of our own victories over the French, perhaps we should be more aware of its significance. First, 4,000 Mexican soldiers were greatly outnumbered by the well-equipped French army of 8,000, which had not been defeated for almost 50 years. Secondly, since the Battle of Puebla, no country in the Americas has been invaded by any other European military force. While we named a railway station after one of our victories over the French, Cinco de Mayo is the name of a grand avenue in Mexico City, as well as streets and even villages elsewhere in Mexico. Certainly the day is something to be proud of, though some of the celebrations, at least in the USA, can be a bit tacky.

The Times **Lord Coe** 10 Nov

Sir, I cannot agree with your leading article ("Coe's Toughest Race", Nov 10) that Lord Coe should lead root and branch reform to the administration of international athletics. Had he been a vice-president of the International Association of Athletics Federations (IAAF) for a couple of years, it might be generous to say that he was getting his feet under the table and was keeping his counsel. But with eight years in the appointment, it is disingenuous to say that now as President he has to break from institutional loyalties and act in this way. Lord Coe should indeed move quickly and step down in favour of someone untainted by this episode and offer anything he knows about it; then, if appropriate, offer himself for election again to IAAF, or any new body that might emerge.

DTel **Ordinals ahead of their time** 12 Nov

SIR - The contemporary inscription at the foot of the chalice in the Portland collection which begins "King Charles the First" (Letters, November 12) reminded me of an illustration I once saw on the cover of a historical novel: a Yeoman Warder had emblazoned on the front of his Tudor uniform, "E I R".

DTel **Speeding stigma** 16 Nov

SIR - Barbara Davy asks what it is that makes non-compliance with speed limits so acceptable when other law-breaking and life-threatening activities are not (Letters, November 16), citing a motorist telling her he had covered much of a long motorway journey at about 90mph. Motorways are the safest of all our roads and the driver's journey was presumably victimless, even from increased emissions, and assuming that the car had not been stolen. Far from being acceptable, though, is the breaking of speed limits on roads below 40 mph, which accounts for more than two thirds of accidents in which people are killed or seriously injured and so is not generally boasted about.

The Times   19 Nov

Nuclear option

Sir, Marjorie Ellis Thompson, the former chair of CND (letter, Nov 18), is wrong to claim that the theory of deterrence has not been tested in any wars in which we have been involved. Not only was it tested throughout the Cold War, which saw by far the largest commitment for HM Forces during the period (1947 - 1991), but it worked. The Berlin Wall came down and the Iron Curtain went up without the direct use of armed force by either adversary. MALCOLM WATSON (Colonel, ret'd)

| *The Times* | **Pub lunches** | 20 Nov |

Sir, Robin Crane (letter, Nov 20) omitted one key item of food from those historically offered by most pubs - crusty bread - which together with cheese forms the basis of the Ploughman's Lunch and predates any pub lunch spawned by the 1967 Road Safety Act and the introduction of the breathalyser test.

| *Evening Standard* | | 23 Nov |

(Get real, Mr Clegg)

Nick Clegg writes [Comment, November 19] that we must not let terrorist attacks turn countries inwards and away from each other, but the government's first duty is to protect its citizens, and while this may require turning inwards, it does not mean turning away from other countries. Look at our relations with France – I don't think we have ever been closer.

Too heavily edited to highlight.

The Times **Flatulent expenditure** 27 Nov

Sir, I do hope that no decisions are taken on our future diet (report, Nov 24 & letter, Nov 27), as contributions to combat global warming, until the results have been analysed from Colombia where the Department of Energy and Climate Change is spending £15 million of our taxes over four years to monitor flatulent cows and reduce greenhouse gas emissions from cattle ranching.

Evening Standard **Melting away** 28 Nov

The subterranean scramble to eke out space below town houses is indeed only the tip of the iceberg [Leading article, "Downward mobility",Nov 27], especially when compared to the building of a four-storey basement beneath the listed former hotel a stone's throw from Buckingham Palace [Business, "Palace coup", Nov 27). However, the joint forces of nature and the law won't "sink the icebergs in the end" as icebergs float; they must combine to apply heat to ensure they melt away.

DTel **Hats on** 29 Nov

SIR - I have always religiously taken my hat off whenever I have needed to enter church while my wife does her turn with the church flowers, sometimes days before the heating is turned on for a service.   As a follically challenged man I shall now keep my hat on and make sure I have at hand Jeremy Goldsmith's letter (November 27) in case challenged there to remove it.

The Times   **Davis Cup stamps**   30 Nov

Sir, David Lamming (letter, Nov 30) omitted the first special stamp to celebrate our sporting success, England winning the football World Cup in 1966. His suggestion for Davis Cup victory stamps could be introduced into next year's Royal Mail schedule most memorably if they were issued to coincide with Wimbledon, the site of the 1936 Davis Cup final, 80 years on from that victory and 50 years after the Wembley triumph. It will also be the 80th anniversary of the death of royal philatelist, King George V.

Evening Standard   **'O', what a slip**   1 Dec

Sir Max Hastings would, of course proverbially, have been kicking an Old Carthusian when he was down, not an old Carthusian [Sam Leith, November 30], a slip that would not have occurred under his editorship.

The Guardian   **Cricket club closures**   2 Dec

Rupert Litherland of Winslow CC has my sympathy along with the others forced to close cricket clubs through lack of players ("A small club in big trouble", December 1), but we should not be surprised. The youngest of those captivated by the 2005 Ashes victory would now be coming through to play senior cricket after leaving school, but the lack of free-to-air TV in every home and shop window has left the vast majority with insufficient coverage to sustain their interest.

I cannot imagine my teenage years without being able to watch Test cricket on TV, then going outside to emulate the strokes and bowling actions of the great players of the day, leading to my playing the game at a good standard for over 30 years. We can only hope that advances in technology will make some form of free-to-air a reality again, sooner rather than later, if cricket clubs are not to close at the same rate as pubs.

DTel   **Syria**   4 Dec

SIR - Fraser Nelson should not have included Sierra Leone to give some credence to liberal interventionism ("Awful though it seems, working with Assad may be the only option", December 4) as British troops were sent there for an operation to evacuate non-combatants. Otherwise his analysis of the complex situation surrounding Syria has parallels with solving complex mathematical equations, where a technique known as fixing the variables is used. The sooner that the coalition partners agree to President Assad remaining in power, albeit for the time being, the easier it will be to pursue a credible and lasting solution.

Sunday Times　　　　**HIGNFY***　　　　6 Dec

A special thank you to Karl Bundy for revealing mine and it would seem the prevailing ignorance of others about Kathy Burke. I certainly had no idea about her talents or even what she looks like, not least as I missed that particular HIGNFY.

* Have I Got News for You

Evening Standard　　　　8 Dec

(The price of peace)

Jane Eades asks "when has aggression ever brought peace?" [Letters, December 4). Lest we forget - and so soon after Remembrance Day - the allies in the First and Second World Wars brought peace through force of arms and sacrifice, not through pacifism and surrender.

Daily Telegraph   9 Dec

Heathrow heads*

SIR - The Government is not shying away from taking a controversial decision on London's airport capacity.

It is trying, quite properly, to ensure that it takes the right controversial decision for the right reasons.

*Refers to the letter above mine which called on David Cameron to have heads for Heathrow, tails for Gatwick.

The Times   **Lessons recorded**   11 Dec

Sir, CDs are not just being played for entry and exit music at church weddings (letter, Dec 11), but tapes as well for the music accompanying hymns at Sunday church services. In keeping with the virtual organist, I have offered to record some lessons to save the local churchwardens feeling they have to read so many.

An accompanying hologram at the lectern may be a bit presumptive, but who knows what lies ahead for the established church?

Private Eye   **Commentatorballs**   12 Dec

"Mackerel can be very fishy."
MIKE GATTING, BBC2 (Masterchef: The Professionals)

DTel   **Heathrow et al**   18 Dec

SIR - Sir Nigel Rudd, the Heathrow chairman who has announced his retirement next September, says that the decision on London's airport capacity has been thrown into the long grass (Business, December 18), when it is still clearly visible above the winter cut along with the toys from his pram. Together with the CBI, they seem to think that those who shout the loudest will win the day.

The Government is, quite rightly, not going to be bullied into submission when Sir Howard Davies, the Airport Commission's chairman, has admitted to Parliament that "Clearly some things have moved on. The Government will need to satisfy itself that this can be done safely".

The Times **Retired professionals** 18 Dec

Sir, I can't help noticing that the number of correspondents who are emeritus professors seems to exceed by far the number of professors. Are professors restricted in commenting on their fields of expertise as serving officers are, or do those who have retired just have more time on their hands and confidence in what they wish to share?

MALCOLM WATSON (Colonel, ret'd)

DTel **Mental English** 21 Dec

SIR - Should those of us having difficulty imagining what a "unique cross-sector peer-to-peer mentoring programme" is be worried about our mental health (Letters, December 21), or just those who admit it?

DTel **Downton Abbey spin-offs** 27 Dec

SIR - As "Matthew is killed in a car crash, just after the birth of his first son" (News, No 2 of "Downton's memorable moments", December 26), there may still be more surprises ahead as the miraculous conceptions of other sons come to light in spin-off series.

DTel   **The price of a pint**   29 Dec

SIR - Anyone paying £4 or more in a pub for a pint containing three or more units of alcohol (Letters, December 29) is clearly prepared to do so and for strong beer around 5% alcohol by volume (ABV). Fortunately, those not committed to eat there, or willing to pay such prices, can go elsewhere.

Nowadays, brewers are producing many more good beers around 3.5% ABV (just over 2 units of alcohol) for landlords to offer discerning drinkers at lower prices. One such beer is regularly sold for £1.99 a pint in J. D. Wetherspoon pubs, where it can also be enjoyed free of any background music, as well as smoke.

Drafted but not sent:

The Times   *Double entendres*   *31 Dec*

Sir, Carol Midgely is right to challenge those so easily offended by names such as the Black Cock *inn (Times2, Dec 30), though having done so my attention was drawn during the local production of* Dick Whittington *that evening to a placard with the message "I love Dick". The context of the scene with the young girl carrying it was rather lost on me, but perhaps it shouldn't have been.*

2016

The Times   **11 and 12 times tables**   5 Jan

Sir, Any readers completing the Brain Trainer
exercises in Mind Games last month will have used
the 11 and 12 times tables during the last 20 days,
never mind the last 20 years (letter, Jan 5). Dividing
by 11 and 12 (Times2, Dec 21, 23, 28) requires the
application of that part of the tables in order to do so.

DTel   **Online publication**   6 Jan

SIR - Professional writers, far from becoming an
"endangered species", should be looking to
themselves - not their publishers - to secure their
survival through self-publishing online ("Poor pay for
e-books 'putting off authors'", News, January 6).

  Publication of both print and e-books costs nothing
and royalties are set by the author and can be paid
monthly. Online customers can browse a selection of
books larger than in any bookshop and can read the
first few pages before purchase; e-books are delivered
instantly, print versions within a day or two and both
are of high quality.

  This is the future of publishing and it is publishers
and agents, along with bookshops, that are the
endangered species.

Evening Standard   **History and corrections**   7 Jan

Andrew Lloyd Webber and Tim Rice did not feel
obliged to correct history with their letter to *The Times*
about the late Robert Stigwood [Londoner's Diary,
January 7], they wanted to correct a bit of the content
in his obituary.

DTel   **Charges for use of a debit card**   8 Jan

SIR - I have just been charged 0.5 per cent on top of an
insurance premium to pay it using a debit card.
Apparently it costs nothing to pay by cheque, but it
would not have cleared before the cover was
required. I wonder if any other readers have been
faced with this seemingly regressive step in the
marketplace?

The Times   **Cringe drinking?**   8 Jan

Sir, As these latest guidelines seem designed in part
to make the consumption of alcohol less socially
acceptable, will those choosing to ignore them be
considered to be cringe drinking?

The Spectator   9 Jan

In with Ginge

Sir: It will be news to many of those who served with, or under the command of, the late Field Marshall Sir Nigel Bagnall that his nickname when out of earshot was Baggie (Drink, 2 January). Throughout the army he was referred to as Ginge, on account of his hair. This is also borne out by the existence of an unofficial thinktank he convened aside from the chain of command, but reaching down a rank level or two to encourage talent for the future. *Made up of like-minded warrior innovators*,* It was known as the Ginger group by those who may or may not have been invited to be members of it.
Col J.M.C.Watson (retired)

*Edited out.

Sunday Times   10 Jan
Sport section

(First balls both ways)

If Michael Slater's searing cut shot to the first ball of the 1994-95 Ashes series punctured the opposition's collective optimism (Ed Smith, Jan 3), Steve Harmison's first ball wide to second slip in the 2006-07 series had the reverse effect. *Australia going on to win the first match and then the series both times*.*

*Edited out.

DTel   **The question of David Bowie**   13 Jan

SIR - I am grateful for the extensive media coverage of the life and work of David Bowie, as his apparent influence had completely passed me by (Letters, January 12 and 13). I now feel confident in at least being able to understand, if not answer, a quiz question about him.

The Times   **"That's what it's all about."**   14 Jan

Sir, I agree with Gordon Turner* (letter, Jan 14) that we are second to none for self-deprecation, though my take on it was to suggest *Hokey Cokey* in response to the call for music to accompany the Radio 4 PM programme's pieces during the final run up to the In-Out EU referendum.

*He had proposed the Hokey Cokey *for the English national anthem.*

DTel   **Easter Day**   18 Jan

SIR - Michael Fielding is right that Britain passed an Act in 1928 to fix the date for Easter (Letters, January 18) and it reads: "Easter-day shall, in the calendar year next but one after the commencement of this Act and in all subsequent years, be the first Sunday after the second Saturday in April." It requires only an Order in Council for it to begin and includes a year's delay to offset the Archbishop's concern about the advanced printing of calendars, if not his alternative of the third Sunday, should that be the decision (Report, January 16).

Sunday Times **David Bowie** 19 Jan

I have been intrigued by the extensive media coverage of the life and work of David Bowie, culminating in your colourful 10-page tribute (Culture, Jan 17), as his apparent influence had completely passed me by. However, I now feel confident enough to understand, if not answer, a quiz question about him.

The Times **Men's haircut options** 20 Jan

Sir,   What are a unisex salon and a blow dry (letter, Jan 20*)?

*Apparently a woman "can go to a unisex salon and pay £20-25 for a cut and blow dry, while a man having the same will be charged £15."

DTel **National costume** 21 Jan

SIR - There are a number of forms of dress which could lay claim to be our national costume, but none recognisable by all (Letters, January 21). This could easily be remedied with the addition of pull-on armlets of tattoos or removable transfers on the neck (as needed), making the connection obvious - both at home and abroad.

The Times   **Tuppence for a suitor**   22 Jan

Sir,   As Tuppence is the nickname for Prudence,
Tuppence Middleton could arguably be better off
being introduced to a member of the Farthing family
(letter, Jan 21*).

**A correspondent had suggested "for the sake of happy
nomenclature — of introducing her to the equally brilliant
Wales rugby star Leigh Halfpenny?"*

The Times   **Fathers and sons cricket matches**   24 Jan

Sir,   Though Stephen Cook scoring a hundred for
South Africa against England is the second instance of
a player scoring a hundred on Test debut when his
father recorded a duck on the same occasion (Sport,
Jan 23), they remain the only father and son to have
made triple centuries in first-class cricket: Jimmy
Cook, 313 for Somerset in 1990; Stephen Cook, 390 for
Lions in 2009.

The Times   **Golf's dress code**   24 Jan

Sir, Giles Smith is quite wrong to say that shorts have
no place in golf (Sport, "Short shrift for golf's new
dress code", Jan 23). Tailored shorts have long been
allowed for gentlemen on even the smartest golf
courses, making them the coolest players during the

hottest weather, but only when worn with knee-high socks.

<table>
<tr><td>*DTel*</td><td>**War and Peace uniforms**</td><td>27 Jan</td></tr>
</table>

SIR,   The BBC may have found creating many different uniforms for their adaptation of *War and Peace* prohibitive (News, Jan 26), but those that do feature are not always worn correctly. The pelisse, or short jacket of the light cavalry worn in the manner of a short cloak, should hang loosely from over the left shoulder. Young Nikolai Rostov seems uncertain as to which side it should be, or at least his dresser is.

But see 14 Feb.

<table>
<tr><td>*The Guardian*</td><td>**Dad's Army**</td><td>28 Jan</td></tr>
</table>

Peter Bradshaw's review of the latest Dad's Army film, read online, cued me to click on the trailer ("Dad's Army review: who don't you think you are kidding?", Jan 26). It includes the funny moment Bradshaw mentions when Captain Mainwaring appears in his Churchillian garb. Readers expecting to see him in a homburg, though, will be disappointed - he is wearing his bowler hat. The Oxford-educated Sergeant Wilson, of course, wears a homburg to work in the television series.

| *The Times* | **Egham municipal** | 1 Feb |

Sir, So much then for Sunningdale members referring to Wentworth golf club as Egham municipal ("Wentworth members pitch for court over £100,000 joining fee", News, Feb 1).

| *The Times* | **'inge drinking** | 1 Feb |

Sir, For those us, like Peter Young (letter, Feb 1), who will continue to take our chances in greater levels of imbibing in direct and knowing defiance of the chief medical officer's advice, I offer the following definitions: fringe drinking - drinking within the old guidelines in public; cringe drinking - drinking within the new guidelines in public, while continuing to drink within the old guidelines at home; tinge drinking - keeping within the new guidelines at home; whinge drinking - complaining about the new drinking guidelines, while holding a drink.

Daily Telegraph   3 Feb

Worrying development

SIR - Thank you to Christopher Howse for his revelations about the growing use of the phrase "no problem" (Comment, February 2).

I recently asked a member of staff on a hospital ward to stop using its variant, "no worries", during a conversation about my father, as, while she may not have had any, I did.

Her immediate response was: "No worries."

Evening Standard   3 Feb

Lawson's Google tax wouldn't work

Lord Lawson knows better than to imagine that multi-national companies can simply be taxed on UK sales. Such a sales or "turnover" tax could not be imposed unilaterally as a member of the EU, where VAT provides a measure of these.

To do so after leaving the EU would be unhelpful to UK businesses and mark an unwelcome return to protectionism, while playing into the hands of the multi-nationals, as well as other nations.

The Times   **Whose road?**   5 Feb

Sir, Lady Powell notes that in the New Forest near her, where there are no white lines, drivers definitely slow down when faced with oncoming traffic in the middle of the road (letter, Feb 5). Unfortunately, the same does not always apply to drivers travelling in the same direction. On Tuesday, near her home, not even an oncoming police vehicle deterred a driver from overtaking us well in excess of the 40 mph limit for the area. The removal of white lines has unintended consequences.

DTel   **Pre-war pilot**   6 Feb

SIR - May I add my own adventure to those of your other correspondents (Letters, 3, 5, 6).

In 1934, aged 14, living in Brough in the East Riding of Yorkshire, where the Blackburn Aeroplane & Motor Company had a factory, my father was friendly with the managing director and also Wing Commander Loton, the chief test pilot, who arranged for me to be flown in the naval Blackburn Dart trainer, with floats fitted, sitting in front of the pilot. I remember being lowered down the slipway into the

River Humber and taking off towards Hull in an easterly direction. The flight took about an hour and we circled the two forts at the mouth of the Humber and, on returning to Brough, we were hauled up the slipway by a farm tractor.

I also flew in a Blackburn B2 trainer, in which the pilot and trainee sat side by side, and we looped the loop on that same fine day.

John Watson
Ryde, Isle of Wight

Written by and sent for my father.

DTel   **Free movement of EU citizens**   8 Feb

SIR - Boris Johnson writes that, until recently, "free movement" within the EU applied to "workers" and not all EU citizens (Comment, February 8).

Interestingly, the Supreme Court held as recently as January 27 that a citizen of another EU member state who moved to the UK but was not a worker, job-seeker, student, self-employed or self-sufficient could be validly denied a right of residence here.

Perhaps this will help inform one of the answers Mr Johnson seeks about the Tusk 'deal'.

Sunday Times   **Vote appropriate**   11 Feb

I cannot agree with Jack Siviour that those of us over
65 years old should not have a vote in the EU
referendum (Letters, February 7). I was young when I
voted back in 1975 and if I had known then the
consequences of our choice I would not have voted as
I did. I for one wish to make amends.

Evening Standard   12 Feb

(Democracy in London)

Stan Labovitch is wrong to say that
democracy doesn't work unless everyone
takes part [Letters, February 9]. It also
works when the will of the majority is
accepted by minorities, including those who
feel no need or wish to vote, for whatever
reason.

A divided party

SIR - James Willis (Letters, February 10) asks if the EU and its predecessors have managed to get anything right.

I nominate euro banknotes. Printed in convenient sizes in seven denominations with imaginative designs in a variety of colour schemes (including visual security features) they are made of pure cotton fibre *which improves their durability and gives them their distinctive feel**.

Here in Britain, three of our four denominations are to be printed on polymer, though the future of the £50 note has yet to be decided.

*Edited out.

The heading referred to three letters above mine about the Conservative Party and the EU.

Sunday Times   14 Feb
Culture section

(War and Peace uniforms)

The pelisse, or short jacket of the light
cavalry, when worn in the manner of a
short cloak, should hang loosely from over
the left shoulder. By wearing it on both
sides, Nikolai Rostov seems to have been
unaware of this.

Evening Standard   **Cyclists**   15 Feb

Stuart Hulls may well be right that London's reckless
cyclists show utter contempt for pedestrians and road
users [Letters, February 12], but what they really
show utter contempt for is the Highway Code. If they
abided by it, others should have nothing to fear from
them.

Country Life   **Spot the Difference**   17 Feb

Like many other readers I turn first of all to Tottering-
By-Gently for its true-to-life insights, but I wonder if
Annie Tempest has come up with a new and
wonderful way to entertain us - Spot the Difference.

Look again in the February 17 issue: at the picture on the wall of his lordship fishing, the child's drawing, the Peppa Pig, the Dalek and the teddies. Any advance on 20, or the chance of a competition, perhaps in aid of charity?

The Times	**Vaping and older smokers**	18 Feb

Sir, Professor Balls and Dr Combes say that quitting smoking by taking up vaping may be laying the foundations for a public health disaster, albeit one that may not become apparent for decades (letter, Feb 18).

Never having smoked, I took to Cuban cigars 18 years ago at the age of 50, without any desire to inhale. Last year I enjoyed a smoke with a cricketing acquaintance who had taken up smoking cigarettes at the age of 70.

Older smokers moving to vaping, like hitherto non-smokers discovering the pleasures of smoking occasionally in later life, are unlikely to trouble the scorers in the remaining decades of their lives. Is no one exempt from such scaremongering?

The Times	**The use of the name Jesus**	23 Feb

Sir, When we lived in Mexico City, our gardener was called Jesús, pronounced *Heh-SOOS*. He had the right attitude and performed miracles using the tools he favoured.

DTel **In/Out and the EU** 24 Feb

SIR – If in doubt,/It must be Out.

The Times **Wrong line** 24 Feb

Sir, S I Redstone is mistaken about the pigeons travelling on the Piccadilly line (letter, Feb 24), which is subterranean at Earls' Court and does not go to Putney Bridge. It would have been on the District line.

The Cricketer **Donning the right pullover** 24 Feb

Mike Selvey's article (March 2016 issue) on the wearing of different regalia, prior to 1998, by England's Test players at home and abroad brought to mind the case of Yorkshire spinner, the late Don Wilson, who played five Test matches against India and one against New Zealand, all abroad. He was also capped by England in the series against the Rest of the World in 1970 and wore the St Edward's crown and three lions; but two years later the International Cricket Council declared that they should not be regarded as Test matches.

When in 1977 he was appointed by MCC as Head Coach he could frequently be seen wearing his England pullover in the new indoor school and at matches with the MCC Young Cricketers. It took till 1980 for the records of the matches to be removed from *Wisden* (against the wishes of the editor, Norman Preston), but it would have taken much more to wrest the England regalia from this proud recipient. *See page 202.*

The Times	**The Queen's 90th**	26 Feb

Sir,   What a pity that the price of the tickets for the Queen's 90th birthday picnic couldn't have been pegged at an eye-catching £90 rather than an eye-watering £150 ("Extra tickets for the Queen's party", Feb 26).

Daily Telegraph	29 Feb

Courts could well sit in libraries instead of pubs

SIR - Libraries would seem to offer viable alternative venues to hotels and pubs for court sittings (Letters, February 27).

In the late Seventies I sat as a captain on a court martial in Portadown, Northern Ireland, when the proceedings were constantly interrupted by helicopter activity near the courtroom. In the end, the presiding judge called for the convening officer and demanded that the court be relocated, as he was unable to concentrate on his summing-up. We reconvened the following day and discharged our duties in the quiet of the large library in the barracks at Lisburn.

If shared costs and usage could be agreed, being able to conduct sittings in this manner could act as a lifeline for libraries faced with closure.

Col JMC Watson (retd)

The judge went on to become Chief Justice - in the peace and quiet - of the Solomon Islands.

The Oldie   **The bust of Nelson Mandela**   5 Mar

Sir: I used to pass the large bust of Nelson Mandela on the elevated walkway between Waterloo Station and Hungerford Bridge twice a day when I worked in

London in 1985/86 and witnessed the nature of its repeated destruction (Jeremy Lewis, March issue). Once it was discovered that it wasn't made of bronze, but was hollow and painted to look like it over fibre glass, I always felt that it was being continually damaged because it could be and so easily. I wouldn't wish to tempt providence by pointing this out, since a "bronze" replacement returned to its plinth and repositioned alongside the Royal Festival Hall in 2007 has remained intact, but I do wonder if there is any more metal there than there was before.

The Times	**Just so, Supermarket**	6 Mar

Sir, I cannot let your leading article ("Not So Supermarket", Mar 1) go without disagreeing that the immediate effect of the Amazon/Morrisons deal will be to offer consumers "a new way to have cheap food delivered to their doors". It will offer another way to have fresh food delivered to their doors more cheaply.

The Times	**Disastrous pleading**	10 Mar

Sir, It is good to know that so many eminent Cambridge scientists wrote in an individual capacity explaining that if the UK leaves the EU and there is a loss of freedom of movement of scientists between the UK and Europe, it would be a disaster for UK science and universities (News report and letter, Mar 10).

Did it not occur to any of the more than 150 of these Fellows of the Royal Society that by using the word "disaster" their explanation had just the same scaremongering impact as a contrived letter from No 10, or might that be why the other 30% of the Royal Society's fellows from Cambridge didn't join them in signing it?

I await eagerly the carefully considered weighting of all this special pleading being brought together, with other key factors, into coherent conclusions about the long-term interests of this country and the security of its people - both inside and outside the EU - by any individual, group of individuals, or institution capable of producing them. Voters deserve nothing less.

DTel   **Pre-flight checks**   11 Mar

SIR - Let's be fair: *pre-boarding* at the airport (Letters, March 11) is Priority Boarding for *pre-assigned* seats. *Pre-boarding* is about life before boarding school.

A letter had appeared questioning the use of pre-order *in ITV's* Mr Selfridge.

Sunday Times   13 Mar
Culture section

Churchill's Secret was spoilt for me by Sir
Winston being portrayed in the opening
scene during dinner with his starched shirt
front buttoned up the wrong way.
Churchill was no lady's blouse.

Sunday Times   **Wilkinson on TV**   13 Mar
Sport section

Johnny Wilkinson was an outstanding fly-half and
goal kicker for England. As a TV pundit he stands
out for his barely fathomable set-piece answers to
questions that haven't been put to him. He should be
dropped before his reputation suffers any more.

The Times   **Grounds for recycling**   16 Mar

Sir, People are not just being misled about recycling
of paper coffee cups where coffee is sold (report, Mar
15). Bringing in from the car two shiny gold 1 kg bags
inscribed "Waitrose Fairtrade Expresso Beans", I was
surprised to be asked to take them outside again.   It
appears that the coffee grounds used for making
coffee in their stores are available for use in the

garden and can be picked up free of charge, complete
with a Best Before date.

Sunday Times   **You say**   16 Mar
Culture section

Indian Summers: here we go again. The viceroy's car
suddenly switches from right- to left-hand-drive,
officers salute with their left hands and all before the
title has come up on the screen.

DTel   **Roald Dahl's equals**   20 Mar

SIR - Michael Deacon writes that no author knew how
to delight children quite like Roald Dahl did
(Comment, March 19). Maybe not. But it seems
unthinkable for Arthur Ransome, Enid Blyton and
J.K.Rowling not being seen as at least his equal in
their own times and special ways.

The Times   **Shoelaces**   23 Mar

Sir, I have just ordered a product called Easy Laces
which I found in a brochure that has come through
the letterbox (letters, Mar 19, 22, 23). Stretchable
silicon laces in two widths, in black or brown, fit
neatly and securely between the eyelets to turn lace-
up shoes into slip-ons. I can hardly wait to try them -

with the help of my long shoehorn.

I converted three pairs of walking shoes and don't expect to tie shoe laces for them again. Boots are another matter.

| *The Times* | **Batsmen are back** | 26 Mar |

Sir, How reassuring to see Mike Brearley, in his article about the Spirit of Cricket (Sport, Mar 26), eschew the use of the American term "batter" when referring to "Sarah Taylor, the England batsman". That's the spirit!

| *DTel* | **Talking point** | 28 Mar |

SIR - Madeline Helps says Wightlink ferries no longer give her family anything to talk about (Letters, March 28). On our return from a day-trip to the Isle of Wight on Saturday, I tried to keep the ticket under cover from the rain for the day-glow clad official standing ready to inspect it. However, he was unable to extend his arms over the tarmac towards the vehicle due to "health and safety". We spoke of nothing else on the ferry.

DTel   **The music in *Dr Thorne***   29 Mar

SIR - The production team of *Dr Thorne* was also
found wanting with its music for the recent television
series (Letters, March 29). Anthony Trollope's novel
was first published in 1858, while *The Skaters' Waltz*,
which opened the dancing following the sumptuous
wedding breakfast, was composed in 1882. Not quite
such a happy ending after all.

A version published in the Sunday Times, Culture
Section on *10 April will be included in the next volume,*
"Even More Wit and Wisdom..."

DTel   **Pronouncing almonds**   30 Mar

SIR - Everyone on the latest spin-off, *Bake Off: Crème
de la Crème*, seems to say *al-monds*. Come back Mary
Berry (Letters, March 30).

*A correspondent had written in to say that Mary Berry's
cakes seemed to consist of* lairs.

*At which point, the third packet of Wit and Wisdom letters
ends.*

TRAVEL

TRAVEL TOPICS

At the end of September 2013, I saw in *The Sunday Telegraph* travel section, *Discover,* a two-page spread titled *Your say* in which readers are asked to write in with their tips and recommendations on a specified topic, frequently related to a feature article that week. Entries are limited to 150 words and the winning review gets a prize. The first entry I submitted, on Cuba, won* and several others have been published including another winning entry.

In January 2014, I noticed in *The Daily Telegraph* that the Saturday *Travel* section had a similar two-page spread titled *Your travels* in which readers are asked to email relevant feedback, limited to 200 words, on that week's edition. Once again, my first entry won*, a number of others have been published, along with a second winning entry.

What follows are yet more entries submitted, with those published shown in a larger font and the prizes won. They are shown in the format published, with the headings and subscripts as used in each; these have changed during the period with changes to the *Telegraph* papers' formats. As with the letters, (P) indicates that the published entry was accompanied by a photograph.

*See *More Wit and Wisdom of an Ordinary Subject*.

DTel **Napoleon on Elba** 14 Oct 14

What bad luck that Napoleon arrived on Elba "in the May of 2014"; another six months and he could have flown in via Pisa, "courtesy of Silver Air" ("Exile on Elba? If only we had Napoleon's luck", October 11).

Daily Telegraph 1 Nov 14
Travel section

US drive tips

Paul Wander ('Discover the USA on an epic road trip', October 25) lists all the main attractions worth exploring on his drive between San Francisco and Los Angeles, except perhaps one. Santa Barbara, 95 miles from Los Angeles, is a picturesque California mission town facing the Pacific, where bright bougainvillea flowers purple and magenta against the classic white adobe houses and small clapboard buildings recall the 19th century settlers. Wander along the vine-hung hacienda-lined streets of its historic district and stay at the Upham Hotel's Country House, furnished comfortably with antiques.

Second part, which was omitted:

Similarly, on the journey from New York to Boston, take the opportunity to stop in Connecticut at the town of Mystic, which consists of neat rows of sparkling white buildings along the banks of the Mystic River. In the seaport itself are four major historic ships, a working shipyard, a recreated 19th century community area with craftspeople, and a formal exhibition area. After arriving in Boston don't hand back your car until you have ventured 12 miles north to Salem, capital of the Massachusetts Bay Colony from 1626 to 1630, but earning a bitter name in American history as the scene of the witch trials, in which a group of women and children accused 19 villagers of witchcraft.

STel	**Tips on a European city where history comes alive**	3 Nov 14

STOCKHOLM

Arriving at the Berns Hotel, with parts of it dating back to 1863, Stockholm's history came alive. The Vasa Museum houses the remarkably well preserved Vasa - Sweden's Mary Rose - and 24,000 items on board when it sank on its maiden voyage in 1628. The Old Town district, a warren of small buildings, jumbled together in crooked rows, is unmistakably medieval; merchants have traded in the squares since the 13th century. At the Royal Palace, it is the subterranean museum in what remained after the fire of 1697 that gives such a fascinating picture of its nearly 1000 years of history. The striking Östermalm covered food hall offers a taste of typical market trading from the past. Back on the hotel's roof terrace, the spires, domes and buildings panning out below left us in no doubt about the vibrancy of the city's past. During next year's Waterloo bicentenary, try ABBA The Museum.

DTel **Morocco** 10 Nov 14

Tara Stevens ('Making a lot more of Morocco', November 9) could have offered even more charm and intrigue away from Marrakesh by suggesting a drive to Oukaimeden, North Africa's largest ski resort, only 50 miles south, but over 10,000 feet above sea level in the Altas Mountains. Less than an hour and a half away you will be among snow covered pine trees in contrast to the palm trees and red city you left behind. Lift passes are cheap, as is equipment hire. Four drag lifts service the nursery and intermediate slopes and seven chair lifts operate higher up, including the continent's highest, with access beyond it by donkey. Originally developed by the French, Hotel Chez Juju is a lovely spot for lunch and Hotel Le Courchevel for a great bar and welcoming fire. Return to Marrakesh after dark to see the lights of the city as you descend and for a wider choice of après-skiing.

Sunday Telegraph   4 Jan 15
Discover section

Tips on festivals
around the world (P)

THE DAY OF THE DEAD

Weeks before the Day of the Dead in
Mexico on November 2, bakeries and
market stalls are filled with toys and death-
themed sweets such as colourful sugar
skulls and death figures shaped from
marzipan. One of the most moving
observances is held on the island of Janitzio
in Lake Pátzcuarro in the state of
Michoacán. On November 1, when dead
children are remembered, women make
their way to the cemetery after midnight,
laden with baskets of food, incense,
bouquets of bright orange flowers, and
thousands of candles, transforming the
small graveyard behind the church on the
island into a glittering outdoor cathedral.
As the women and children meditate at the
grave sites and the church bells toll, the men

begin the slow steady chants that continue through the night.

Malcolm Watson of Berkshire wins a £500 travel voucher from Supertravel Ski

DTel   **To see or not to see**   12 Jan 15

It was ironic - or perhaps counter-intuitive - for some of the 10 "Great sites to avoid?", as reported on TripAdviser, to feature in the eight-page guide "Voyages of Distinction" on the same day (January 10). I dare to suggest there is another one: African safaris. They can be seen much better on television, as the colour is better; you will always see the animals in close-up; and you will invariably see a kill. But seeing is believing and those with funds and time will wish to make their own judgements.

If you go to the southern rim of the Grand Canyon, do not miss the opportunity though to see the 34 minute IMAX film and discover what would otherwise take a lifetime to experience; but in any case have a look at the trailer at http://explorethecanyon.com/imax-theater/imax-movie/ and you can sample flying over and through it from the comfort of your own home.

Sunday Telegraph   15 Feb 15
Discover section

Tips on stately homes
in Britain or Europe

SCHLOSS NYMPHENBURG, GERMANY

A prince's present to his wife for the birth of
an heir, Schloss Nymphenburg lies just west
of Munich in a 495-acre park with lakes,
pavilions and hunting lodges, and was once
the summer residence of the Bavarian kings.
The breathtaking facade of the baroque
complex, which is around 700m (2,300ft)
long, fronts a geometric mix of basins,
canals, hedged paths and lawns. The
opulent great hall is unforgettably
decorated with frescoes and a giant ceiling
painting depicting the Olympian gods. To
the rear, the forest-like parkland has been
reconfigured in the style of an English
landscape garden and makes a spectacular
excursion in late spring when the
rhododendrons and azaleas are in bloom.
Don't miss the south wing, which houses
the world's most important collection of

gilded coaches, state carriages, sleighs and harnesses for every conceivable purpose, as well as a display of exquisite items from the Nymphenburg porcelain factory.

Daily Telegraph   21 Feb 15
Travel section

Log cabins in the US

The myriad of operators listed with the enticing feature "On the road and living the US dream" (February 14) is comprehensive for vehicle and route possibilities, but light on accommodation options. The dream also includes an element of experiencing the great outdoors and Camping Cabins – between camping under canvas and a motel – provide just that excitement without the misery of erecting tentage in the rain.

Found at the sites of Kampgrounds of America (koa.com), the basic log cabin includes a double bed and two bunk beds all with protected mattresses, a table and chairs, and a covered porch. You are required to provide the bedding: we took sleeping bags and pillows.

Many sites have washing and laundry facilities and shops and some even have swimming pools; depending on the location, the cabins also have heating and air-conditioning, as well as a barbecue and space for parking alongside.

While the great highways and national parks are an undoubted pull, using these cabins offers opportunities to venture off the beaten track and breaks from driving taken in state parks can be just as memorable, especially if they have a beach by the ocean, or by an inland lake, as we found in Connecticut and Vermont.

Jane and Malcolm Watson

STel   **Tips on Canada**   23 Feb 15

VICTORIA, BRITISH COLUMBIA
Victoria, the capital of British Columbia, is the province's sunniest city, has Canada's warmest winter and a familiar feel. Stroll around the inner harbour, encircled by the Empress Hotel, the Royal British Columbia Museum and provincial Legislature.

Spot the red letter boxes and our once familiar red telephone kiosks before hopping on a red double-decker bus for a tour further afield. The parks' system offers everything from totem poles to butterflies and a replica of Anne Hathaway's cottage and gardens. Beacon Hill Park with its graceful trees, lakes and bridged streams, also has a century-old cricket pitch. If you are truly adventurous, make for the lookout at Mount Tolmie Park, from where you can overlook 150 years of development, which started as Fort Victoria, the Hudson's Bay Company's most distant outpost in 1843. This 360 degree vista seen from a truly spectacular vantage point is most definitely worth the trip.

Two published entries mentioned Victoria in other contexts.

Sunday Telegraph   8 Mar 15
Discover section

Tips on Alpine holidays

VIENNA, AUSTRIA

The Vienna woods, to the west and south of the city, include a vast, unspoiled forest in an area of extraordinary beauty with numerous well-marked trails. There, alone and isolated, stands Mayerling, where on a snowy night in 1889 Crown Prince Rudolf and his lover the Baroness Mary Vetsera committed double suicide in a hunting lodge. The emperor, who had refused to allow the dissolution of his son's unhappy marriage, had the fatal bedroom torn down and a chapel built in its place. A day's excursion can also take you to the ancient and beautiful Cistercian abbey at Heiligenkreutz, through the lovely wooded Helenental and Europe's largest underground lake, Seegrotte, to the vineyards of Perchtoldsdorf and Gumpoldskirchen and past one of the Prince of Liechtenstein's Austrian castles. Before leaving, find one of the rustic taverns (*heurigen*) for a glass of young wine.

STel   **Tips on Britain's best gardens**   11 Mar 15

BRODSWORTH HALL AND GARDENS
Just off the A1(M) near Doncaster, Brodsworth Hall and Gardens is a gem. The extensive gardens have been wonderfully restored by English Heritage to recapture the Victorian spirit as a 'collection of grand

gardens in miniature', with vistas last enjoyed before the First World War. There are dells of ferns and wild roses, meadows of wild-flowers, a maze of paths and bridges, even an archery range with its target house. The romantic views from the restored summer house take in both the pleasure grounds and the formal gardens; among them are the rose garden with an iron pergola and a hundred varieties; and the fountain garden with a three-tiered Italian marble fountain centrepiece and geometric shapes and brilliant colours of the beds, which change twice a year. Via cedar trees and statues, the spacious formal lawns open up to play host once again to croquet players in traditional white clothing.

Daily Telegraph   29 Mar 15
Travel section

Answers on a postcard, please

Anthony Peregrine suggests that postcards are in need of rehabilitation: they already have been for my travels. On a recent visit to Munich, I used my phone to take a photo of a postcard. Without any need to buy the card, stamp it, or find a postbox, I then sent it by email, utilising the hotel's Wi-Fi, to friends in the USA and received an appreciative reply the same day. Of course it won't cheer up the mantelpiece, but we look forward to receiving reciprocal postcards by email during their forthcoming cruise in the Mediterranean. This is the future; though as Peregrine notes about taking your own drink to the hotel bar to top up your glass, if this catches on at the hotel foyer, it will take practice to carry it off smoothly.

The following week a correspondent claimed that there was something sleazy about my "theft" of a postcard and that I must be bonkers if I thought this was the future. Hence:

DTel　　　　　**Not so bonkers**　　　　8 Apr 15

It seems that Michael Loveridge (April 4) may have missed the tongue-in-cheek nature of my feedback (March 28) linking postcards and mini-bars in the light-hearted Lerosbif column (March 21). Perhaps I should have made it clear that I always buy postcards as souvenirs, particularly of views and of pictures in galleries, as those taken by professional photographers and stocked by shopkeepers will always be far better than anything I can take myself. I suggest that it is the ubiquitous use of cameras on mobile phones, even surreptitiously when they are not permitted, that is the real threat to their income.

DTel **Green safari expectations** 21 Apr 15

Mike Unwin (April 18) exposes the advantages and disadvantages of visiting southern Africa in the green or rainy season - particularly between November and March - but remains on the fence. Visitors hoping to see the big cats if they pay to go on safari then are likely to be disappointed and return home feeling that they did not get value for money. However, if they are lucky enough to find themselves in that part of the continent for other reasons, then by all means stay at a lodge on minimum rates and be the only ones there. Our family did just that, thanks to visiting my brother in South Africa, who lent us a car and booked us into the Kruger National Park for three nights, one of which saw a night drive cancelled because of torrential rain. Though we saw some of the larger animals from designated viewing points, other than some warthogs by the side of the road, the vegetation was too high to see many others from the approved routes for cars and certainly no lions. In our experience, the disadvantages far outweighed the advantages, but then we were at least able to manage our expectations.

GOFF'S CAYE, BELIZE

If you have visions of a paradise island, but blanch at the thought of being stranded on it, then Goff's Caye is the reality. Just a 30-minute boat ride from mainland Belize, you will discover unspoiled beauty, a powdery white sand beach and aquamarine waters which surround its 1.2 acres. This is the perfect getaway for people of all ages - simply lie under the natural shade of the palm trees. Children can play on the beach and in the shallow waters yet never be out of sight. Snorkelling can be done safely from the shore, with plenty to see for first-timers. A little farther out, in a maximum of 15 feet of water, there are large colourful coral formations and numerous ocean creatures to see, including lionfish and barracuda. There is also a small hut for cooking and shelter, as well as another with a couple of loos. Fantastic!

DTel   **Ferry to Cuba**   11 May 15

I was most interested to read (*Travelnews, In short,* May 9) of the resumption of US-Cuba ferry services after more than half a century. Fifteen years ago I travelled with my wife to Havana by ferry from Cancun. This comfortable overnight journey, with all the usual features of live entertainment, an on-deck swimming pool and rum-based drinks at unbeatable prices, made a pleasant change to my 15 previous visits, all flying in from elsewhere in Mexico. The six-day visit, spent half in Havana and half in Santiago de Cuba (a 500-mile flight away) met all our expectations. But as we approached the last item on our itinerary, a visit to the newly opened museum of Havana Club rum in Old Havana, conveniently opposite the berth for our ship, we were surprised to find that the ship had not arrived. In fact, it hadn't even left Cancun, due to a storm, so we had to stay an extra night before having to fly out the next day. If you are hoping to make the trip from Florida, just understand that the hurricane season, which can last from June 1 to November 30, may not guarantee a return ferry journey as planned.

DTel **Golf in Kerry** 9 Jun 15

Having made it to the Kingdom of Kerry for some golf, then go on to the Dingle peninsula and play at Ceann Sibeal, the most westerly golf course in Ireland and hence Europe. Less expensive and demanding than those on Adam Ruck's Irish round to remember (June 6), the views out to the Blaskett Islands in the Atlantic are simply spectacular and well worth the effort to seek out. While there, don't miss the opportunity to see the beach between Slea Head and Dunmore Head, where scenes for *Ryan's Daughter* were filmed. Stay at the peninsula's chief town of Dingle, with its colourful houses and countless pubs, many of which double as shops. Lying at the foot of a steep slope on the north side of the harbour it is bounded on three sides by hills. It was the main port of Kerry in the old Spanish trading days, and in the reign of Queen Elizabeth I it was important enough as an outpost to merit a protective wall. There's no better place than Dingle to relax and get away from it all and enjoy a pint of Guinness.

The next piece was the first I submitted only knowing about the place and not actually having been there. It was no surprise to me that the winning entry, though not mine, was about this railway journey.

STel   **Rail journeys beyond Europe**   15 Jul 15

Mexico
For a spectacular journey on what is arguably "the world's most scenic railroad", take the Chihuahua-Pacific Railway to the natural wonder that is Mexico's Copper Canyon. An exceptional feat of engineering that travels 420 miles through more than 80 tunnels and over 30 bridges was begun in 1897 and completed by the Mexican government in 1961. The 12- to 16-hour trip from Los Mochis (near the Pacific Ocean) to Chihuahua (south of the Texas border), or vice versa, can be made in a single day, with short stops along the way, to enjoy the views; those of the series of huge, deep gorges surpass even the Grand Canyon in both size and beauty. The best time to go is late

summer or early autumn, after the rainy season, when the landscape is crowned with lush greenery. If you have time, spend a night in rustic comfort in a town en route.

STel   **Countries shaped by communism**   21 Jul 15

Cuba

Visiting Cuba in the late 90s with enough time to travel extensively, a fridge sticker at the foyer of our Havana hotel showing the pristine white sand beach at Santa Lucia caught my eye. A quick look at the map revealed it to be not far from Viñales, our destination that day in the tobacco growing western province of Pinar del Río. Disappointed to find a port black with the deposits of industrial activity, we consulted our map again: the recently marketed resort in the eastern province of Camagüey was a mere 413 miles the other side of Havana. Another 200 miles east along the coast is Moa, the nickel mining town doused in sulphur, as far removed from the land Christopher Columbus described as the most beautiful place he had ever seen. These contrasts with the tourist trail, now rightly being promoted, will never leave me.

The next piece of feedback was the second to be written about without having been to the place concerned or having previous knowledge of the subject. This time it was published:

Daily Telegraph   22 Aug 15
Travel section

Borneo's orang-utans

Listing Brunei Airlines among her favourites and praising the Brunei people, Kellie Maloney (Travelling life, August 15) gives the impression that orang-utans can be seen in that country.   Their rainforest home on the island of Borneo does not actually extend to those parts of it on the northern coast that comprise the Sultanate of Brunei, though Brunei can make an excellent base for onward travel.

   The neighbouring Malaysian states of Sabah and Sarawak offer the best chances of seeing orang-utans in their natural habitat, along with proboscis monkeys and pigmy elephants. These states offer better tourist facilities than the southern, Indonesian part of Borneo which is, though, much cheaper and offers far greater scope for non-commercial, off the beaten track travel.

The Borneo orang-utan is listed as endangered as the result of illegal logging and poaching. There are now only 40,000 left in the wild. Patience is required for anyone who wants to see them, as their habitats are a challenge to reach – you will have to use local air transport and the final legs will sometimes be by boat – and wild orang-utans spend their entire lives in trees.

DTel　　　**Knowing the ways to San José**　　8 Sep 15

British Airways (BA) knows the way to San José, according to Travel News (August 29), where it was revealed that the airline is beginning non-stop flights to San José (SJC) in California's Silicon Valley on May 4 2016, but not from where: it's Heathrow (LHR). Readers would be advised to know their way there too, as BA is also beginning non-stop flights that same day to San José (SJO), Costa Rica, but from Gatwick (GAT). Anyone making a booking to either San José should take extra care with the 3-letter airport codes (shown in brackets) as, although the departure airports are only 45 miles apart, there are 3000 miles between the two destinations.

STel   **What for you evokes**   14 Sep 15
          the spirit of Africa?

Driving from north of Johannesburg to the Kruger
National Park takes five hours, plenty of time to take
in the wide open spaces and admire some of the
Drakensberg mountains as we skirted them on our
route. Disappointed that our out of season visit was
hampered by torrential rain making the animals
difficult to see from our car, we stopped during a
break in the weather at a water hole. Then, some 200
yards away a magnificent bull elephant appeared out
of some trees, its graceful gait making us imagine that
what we were watching was being played in slow
motion. I am fortunate enough to have been to
Morocco, Egypt and Kenya in other parts of Africa
seeing there some different landscapes, cultures and
animals, but for me the spirit of that continent is
evoked in the very being of the African elephant.

STel   **Ancient sites and ruins**   23 Sep 15

Toniná is a little-known picturesque site in the hills
between Palenque and San Cristobal in the state of
Chiapas. It is at a higher altitude than Palenque or
Tikal, so is much drier, with a cool breeze and is far
less crowded - when we visited, we were the only
ones there. It centres on an enormous grassy plaza
and a series of seven artificial terraces climbing the
hillside above it. It had been thought that this

acropolis had been built on a hill, but recent excavations have shown that the mound covers the largest pyramid in Mexico - even taller than Teotihuacan's Pyramid of the Sun - and have uncovered a Maya city twice as large as predicted. More than 300 hieroglyphic texts have also been found, revealing the names of the city's rulers; and the texts could eventually help scholars understand the still mysterious decline of the ancient Maya civilization.

STel	**Art in Berlin**	6 Oct 15

During the division of Germany, the 19th century paintings that had survived the war in Western zones of occupation were housed in the Neue Nationalgalerie and Schloss Charlottenburg's Gallery of Romanticism in the British sector of West Berlin, where I served before the fall of the Berlin Wall. Returning 30 years later to find the growing collections united in their original building, now called Alte Nationalgalerie on Museum Island in what was the Soviet sector, had a special poignancy for me. The current collection includes works of masters such as Adolf von Metzl, Max Lieberman and Arnold Böcklin. Other works include paintings by the Nazarene Brotherhood and the French impressionists. But a visit to Berlin must also include Potsdam on the outskirts to see the stunning Picture Gallery next to Sanssouci Palace with works by Rubens, Van Dyke, and others - all hidden behind the Iron Curtain for so long.

Daily Telegraph   31 Oct 15
Travel section

From Sölden with love (P)

Fifty years ago, I went on a school ski trip during the holidays to Sölden in Austria, the location for *SPECTRE's* spectacular filming in the Alps ("The world is just enough", October 24). Arranged by Erna Low, travel was by train, and her holidays and house parties there, her first destination, were the forerunner of the chalet holiday. I can still ski in my mind the nursery run from the top of a T-bar lift, which I never completed without falling. Having since lived in Mexico City over three Days of the Dead, the filming in the Zócalo there brings back many memories, but the urge is to get out my recently renewed passport and take it to Sölden - by

train, of course – and I might even try to get down the nursery run in one piece.
MALCOLM WATSON WINS A £250 VOUCHER FROM RAILBOOKERS

STel   **Memories of Kenya**   11 Jan 16

Cricket tour

Straddling New Year 1981/82 I went on a wonderful cricket tour there, playing in Nairobi, Mombasa and up in the Rift Valley. Travelling mostly by road we suffered the inevitable breakdown of the ubiquitous camper van and the vagaries of a hotel that hadn't yet been completed, but returning from Mombasa to Nairobi by train we savoured the silver service dining car in more comfort. Between matches we took in the Masai Mara, Tsavo and Amboseli parks with a night in the shadow of Mount Kilimanjaro, seeing all the wildlife we could hope for, except the elusive leopard. Back in Nairobi for our last match, I sneaked off during the lunch interval to photograph the leopards at the Animal Orphanage. Returning in time for the resumption of play I avoided a fine, but then I didn't fly over the ground in a biplane like David Gower did later in Australia.

STel   **Great drives in**   25 Jan 16
                Continental Europe

The Corniches of the French Riviera

Between Nice and Menton, a 19-mile trip, you'll drive through mountain passes, or corniches, that compel you to marvel at dramatic views of both sea and shoreline. From Nice take the N7 to the Grande Corniche. The ascent is quick and especially magical views can be enjoyed as you pause briefly at Belvédère d'Eze, La Turbie, Vistaëro and its medieval château, and at Roquebrune-Cap-Martin. The old towns are enchanting and the landscape, superb. On the return trip, take the lower pass (Corniche Inférieure) to enjoy panoramas that include bird's eye views of some of the loveliest resorts in the world. At Beaulieu-sur-Mer you begin to enter the Côte d'Azur. Take a detour to St-Jean-Cap-Ferrat and visit the Rothschild Foundation, set in exquisite gardens, before returning to Nice via the picturesque town of Villefranche, the classic model of a Mediterranean fishing port, with cliffs that seem to fall into the sea.

STel   **Travelling in Japan**   16 Feb 16

Expo '70

In April 1970, I arrived in Kobe harbour, courtesy of HMS *Bulwark*, on a visit by the carrier to coincide with Expo '70 in Osaka. Within 20 minutes of docking, a Royal Navy mini had been landed on the quay, fitted with Japanese registration plates and four of us were driving along the road - to my great surprise - on the left hand side. So began five unforgettable days at the world exposition and the environs, enjoying activities ranging from admiring the temples and gardens of Kyoto to learning the etiquette of the bathhouse. I well remember a highlight of the fair being a large moon rock on display in the United States' pavilion, brought back from the moon by Apollo 12 astronauts in 1969; seeing there the first-ever IMAX film and wondering at demonstrations of early mobile phones, local area networking and maglev (magnetic levitation) train technology.

EXTRAS

Private Eye   **Pseuds corner**   6 Oct 14

"When fiction writers consider environmental apocalypse, still, they tend to do so with a plunge. I think of that haunting, terrible passage at the end of Cormac McCarthy's *The Road*, and its almost unbearable sadness at the sudden and irrevocable loss of something so simple and wondrous as fish in mountain streams. You don't know quite what has happened, in this stark hell of his, but something has. Something has hit us, bang, and knocked us over the edge."

HUGO RIFKIND on climate change, *The Times*

After my letter was published about eating on buses in London (page10), I followed up with:

Dear Mr Johnson,   11 Oct 14
Thank you for taking the trouble to reply to my email. I quite understand your position and, by the way, agree with the benefits of bus travel you espoused.

   I do believe that what has almost become a "right" to eat on buses could be getting out of hand. Ask someone politely to take their feet, or bags, off a seat, they will almost certainly do so, knowing they are in the wrong; but suggest that they should save eating their meal till they get home and you get a mouthful of abuse as well as food.

I would indeed be interested in a summary from Transport for London (TfL). Thank you for offering to get one.

I received the following reply from TfL via Mr Johnson's assistant on 16 Dec 14:

We actively try to reduce instances of anti-social behaviour such as eating smelly foods through targeted advertising campaigns such as Together for London *and* Travel Better London.

In addition to these campaigns there is a section on our website dedicated to travel etiquette, which Darren's constituent can view at http://www.tfl.gov.uk/campaign/travel-better-london?cid=fs107.

We could not introduce a blanket ban on eating food on the bus as there are some medical conditions that require a person to eat regularly or, in some cases, immediately. We have to be considerate of these customers.

While I'm sorry this isn't the response Darren's constituent may have been looking for, I do hope I have clarified our position on the matter nonetheless.

The Guardian   1 Dec 14

The pictures of the policeman (1892 Paul Martin) and
St Paul's (1840s Anonymous) (Eyewitness, 1
December) are shown reversed, yet they display the
most obvious clues of all those shown as to their
orientation. Are some of the others reversed?

*Thank you for your email about the reversed photos. We
printed them as they were supplied to us by the Science
Museum via the Royal Photographic Society and the
National Media Museum, Bradford. A picture editor
noticed that the numbers on the policeman's tunic and the
St Paul's clock faces were the wrong way round when he
was putting the gallery up on our website and reversed
those two pictures. He says it is a common problem with
glass plate negatives, but we have no way of knowing
whether the other pictures supplied to us are reversed.*

Best wishes, Barbara Harper   *3 Dec 14*

The Spectator   **Competition No 2880:**   17 Dec 14
                           Hard sell

You are invited to compose a publicity blurb for the
bible to sell it to modern audiences. Email entries of
up to 150 words:

"You've seen the films: *The Ten Commandments* (1956),
Ben-Hur (1959), *Samson and Delilah* (1949), *The Robe*

(1953), *The Greatest Story Ever Told* (1965) - all captured in glorious Technicolor. Now, the book behind these and other epic stories from the beginning of time is available online: the King James Bible - the ultimate compilation - in original black and white. Too hefty a tome for most sturdy coffee tables, it has hitherto required a lectern to support it in churches, seats of learning and even in homes. But today, the books of the Old and New Testaments, with their 39 and 27 titles respectively, can be displayed on your computer screen and accessed at the click of mouse. Search by book, chapter and verse. Just go to http://www.kingjamesbibleonline.org/ , where you can also view a mobile version and all at no cost. With colour illustrations accompanying the best known stories."

The Times Feedback	**Correction**	3 Feb 15

Dear Rose,
In Robert Crampton's "Kim and Andy's sweet talk" (Times2, Feb 3), "Hey, Kim, you f***, pass the f***ing salt." and "F***ing have it, you f***." should surely have read "Hey, Kim, you f***er, pass the f***ing salt." and "F***ing have it, you f***er."

True. Perhaps they had stars in front of their eyes.

Rose Wild
Feedback editor
The Times

| *Private Eye* | **Commentatorballs** | 4 Feb 15 |

"The third biggest sporting event in the world is sat on our back door and it's coming around the corner."
STUART LANCASTER, BBC1 News

| *The Times* | **Four more recipes - just** | 3 Mar 15 |
| *Feedback* | | |

Dear Rose,
It is now nearly two years since the publication of the book *The Only Recipes You'll Ever Need* and yet they still keep coming most weeks in Saturday's Magazine. However, as recent offerings have been for spicy cabbage, quick spaghetti and four dishes to use with a tub of pesto, I wonder if you are not scraping the bottom of the pan now. It is difficult to imagine a follow-up title for another compilation, but I am beginning to think that this particular treatment for food may have run its course.

The Spectator   **Competition No 2893:**   8 Apr 15
On the record

You are invited to suggest suitable Desert Island Discs (seven) for a well-known historical figure, living or dead.

My suggestions for King Richard III are:

1. Soundtrack of the film *The Hunchback of Notre Dame* (1939).
2. 'Two Little Boys' by Rolf Harris.
3. 'True Love' by Bing Crosby and Grace Kelly.
4. 'Champion, the Wonder Horse' by Frankie Laine.
5. 'Hole in the Ground' by Bernard Cribbens.
6. 'Dem bones dem dry bones' by Fats Waller.
7. 'My Way' by Frank Sinatra.

Richard III turned out to be the most popular entry and his selections more often than not included 'Dem bones' and 'Two Princes' by the Spin Doctors. The printed entry, among a variety of other figures, also included 'Two Little Boys', but by Sir Harry Lauder.

Private Eye   **Pseuds Corner**   24 Apr 15

"One would need Wagner to orchestrate the fanfare of trumpets which the next wine deserved. 1945, with France in the shadow of war, it was as if Ste Clotilde,

St Louis and Ste Joan d'Arc had implored the Eternal Throne to show mercy. The '45 Bordeaux vintage was the answer to their petition."

BRUCE ANDERSON on Drink, *The Spectator*

The Times *Feedback*	**Correction**	27 Apr 15

Dear Rose,
In today's birthdays, it says that Lady Helen Taylor is "first cousin to the Queen". She is, of course, first cousin once removed to the Queen, her father, the Duke of Kent, being the Queen's first cousin.

A correction was published on 30 Apr 15.

The Times *Feedback*	**Use of the Rt Hon**	28 May 15

Dear Rose,
I am intrigued by the use of the appellation Rt Hon in the list of those attending the Memorial service for Lord Brittan of Spennithorne (Register, May 27). Used for a privy councillor eg. Rt Hon Mr Nick Clegg and Mrs Clegg, the separation indicates that Mrs Clegg is not styled Rt Hon. However used for a privy councillor who is also a baron eg. Rt Hon Lord Waddington and Lady Waddington, the separation is not valid as all barons, viscounts and earls have the

appellation Rt Hon, as do their peeresses. So it should either have been Rt Hon Lord and Lady Waddington, or simply The Lord and Lady Waddington, where The is short for The Rt Hon.

I use as a reference "Titles and Forms of Address, A Guide to Their Correct Use", Thirteenth edition from 1967, but I don't think the basics have changed. I wonder if your Style Guide has introduced some new distinctions?

The Spectator	**Competition No 2902: Howzat!**	2 Jun 15

You are invited to supply a poem incorporating a dozen cricketing terms. Please email entries of up to 16 lines.

How's this?

There are ten ways to get out in cricket,
With one of them known as *Hit wicket*;
Three others, *Bowled, LBW, Caught*,
Each a *duck* if you only score nought.

Run out and *Stumped*, if you're out of your ground,
Will soon have you pavilion bound.
You're there to score runs, but *Hit the ball twice*-
Umpire's finger goes up in a trice.

The last three are still exceedingly rare.
Handled the ball – don't think to go there.
Obstructing the field - not what it's about.
Do either and you'll also be out.

If you're not ready when next in to bat,
Hard it will be if you don't know that
Three minutes can pass before you *take guard*,
Then *Timed out* appears on the scorecard.

The Times   18 Jul 15
Feedback

Dear Rose,
The Daily Universal Register on Saturday incorrectly
refers to the British Open golf championship, after
correctly referring to it as The Open on Thursday.
This matters to those who know these things.

Oh dear, thank you, I've passed it on.

The Times   **Lost property**   28 Jul 15

Sir, Anne Reed's question about the first port of call
for lost property (letter, July 29) and the stories of
kippers as fayre on the railways (letters, July 28, 29)
reminded me of my father, many years ago,
distraught at leaving his briefcase on the train home. I
eventually collected it from the railway lost property

office, identifying myself with knowledge of the
contents: a pair of Manx kippers, which had been
thoughtfully placed in a fridge and the book *How to
Rob Banks without Violence*.
RICHARD SPOONER
Drafted for and sent by my brother-in-law.

Private Eye	**Commentatorballs**	9 Sep 15

"That's what separates these two teams in one-day
cricket, it's that Australia's depth is very broad."
TOM MOODY, Sky Sports 2

| *The Times* | **Correction** | 28 Sep 15 |
| *Feedback* | | |

Dear Rose,
I have earlier this year welcomed the admission of
errors under "Corrections and clarifications" (letter,
May 15), but I feel the tendency to blame the picture
agency for errors in the caption and now for a
photograph reversed is rather unseemly (C&C, Sept
25). Let the buyer beware.
   It cannot be too difficult to expect those calling for
the pictures to know what they are looking at, or for.
In the case of coats being buttoned up differently
between the sexes, the position of medals, buttonholes
and wedding rings, they are simple to learn, if not
always to see. Below is another example of a reversed

photograph* in today's paper (page 42), with the usual clues prominent. It may have come from the agency in that form, but it cannot be their fault for it being published uncorrected here. They may even welcome feedback from you.

Please can we see more care taken with, and responsibility for, picture captions and photograph reversals.

A picture of Captain Blackadder from Series 4.

Yes, it's a fair point. We do always get back to the agency to ask them to correct the errors on their databases. Whether they do or not remains to be seen.

We should also notice these things for ourselves, but in the hurly burly of the night's production they quite often - as you've noticed - get past us.

What I will do is send a note to the picture editors asking them to remind all the picture staff which side medals are meant to go.

Thank you for writing,
Rose

Rose Wild
Feedback editor
The Times

The Times *Feedback*	**Sir, your picture looks annoyingly similar**	3 Nov 15

Dear Rose,

The views of the letters page editor on exclusivity
were clear from your Feedback piece two Saturdays
ago. I wonder what the picture editor feels about
these two photographs in today's papers? Do you not
ask for such scenes to be submitted by readers? As
with the slight alterations in similar letters, I see that
the photographs must have been taken moments
apart and cropped.

Dear Mr Watson,
The photographs are from an agency. We don't, as a rule,
ask readers to submit their own.
Yours,
Rose Wild
Feedback editor
The Times

Thanks for your reply. I confused *The Times* with the
BBC weather on TV which does ask for viewers'
photographs.
MW

Dear Rose,
Your obituary of Major-General Mike Reynolds (Nov
12) *contained the line: "His father worked for Barclays
Bank and his mother stayed at home." This was quite
usual then for someone of his background.** Are we to
expect more such comments from obituary writers,
possibly more familiar with the present than our
past? *Surely, what is worth recording is if such a mother
was employed outside her home, not that she wasn't?** I
am also left wondering whether his own wife
survived him. *(She did, I discovered later).*

*No, it doesn't make much sense. I've passed on to the obits
desk.*
Best wishes,
Rose

Rose Wild
Feedback Editor, The Times

**The content in italics was used later, quoting me, in her
Feedback column on 30 Jan 16.*

| *Evening Standard* | **Errors** | 11 Dec 15 |
| *Editor* | | |

Dear Ms Sands,

I am sure you must have known that Australia does not have an embassy here, but a high commission, though this may be something sub-editors need reminding of too.

I wonder if, in keeping with the other serious daily papers, you might consider having a place for Corrections and Clarifications. I find their admissions of fallibility are both welcome and informative.

Dear Malcolm,

Thank you for pointing out that annoying mistake; I'm sorry it slipped through the net.

We have considered the idea of a corrections column on several occasions. There are clearly pros and cons. For the time being the Standard *is sticking with its customary practice of publishing corrections, as and when they are necessary, on or before the page the original error appeared. We will certainly keep the matter under review.*

Best regards

Will

Will Gore

Deputy Managing Editor

Country Life   **Christmas stamps**   21 Dec 15

Sir, It seems that you have, perhaps inadvertently, awarded the letter of the week (*December 16/23*) on the basis of some misleading information in it about the Christmas stamps revealed in this year's Advent calendar cover (*December 9*). The rate for First Class letters was indeed 3p for Christmas 1972. However, First Class had risen to 8½p for 1975, not 13p, which was the highest value of the four stamps issued for Christmas that year. Also, First and Second Class postage rates were introduced in 1968; the advantage of later stamps just saying 1st or 2nd class is that they can still be used without having to pay any subsequent price rises. It would be churlish to suggest that Linda Bos should return her bottle of champagne for catching your eye during this festive season, but an admission of some fallibility would make a welcome start to the new year.

Silence!

DTel   **Rifkind and Straw**   22 Dec 15

SIR- If "MPs _did_ offer cash for access" (Headline, December 22), then we must be paying them too much. Or did you mean "MPs _did_ offer access for cash"? What a howler!

Private Eye   **MPs offering cash?**   22 Dec 15

What an extraordinary headline in the *Daily Telegraph*! Perhaps they mean "MPs *did* offer access for cash"?

Thank you for your email.   29 Dec 15

The Times   **Corrections and clarifications**   31 Dec 15
Feedback

Dear Rose,

1. In the example of the parlour game Bulls and Cows (Times2, 10 Best Parlour Games, Dec 18), comparing the number 9362 with the fourth number "2436" does not give "1 bull, 2 cows" (getting closer, three are right and one of those is in the correct spot), but "3 cows" (three are right, but none in the right spot).

2. Tasked with barbecuing a whole turkey during the balmy weather this Christmas, Donna Hay's recipe for Barbecued Duck Pancakes caught my eye (Magazine, Dec 18). Now barbecuing can take many forms, but it is always done outdoors and on some form of stand-lone device; this seems to have been done indoors and cooked in an oven. Am I missing something?

Happy New Year!

Yes you're right about both those - it's a mystery why that duck is described as barbequed. I will take it up with the editor of the section.
Happy new year to you too,

Rose

The Times **Corrections and clarifications** 6 Jan 16
Feedback

Rose,
The content following on from the front page article "Ministers forced to back down on Europe" contains the sentence:

> "Mr Cameron did not begin his premiership intending to offer a referendum, and in September party headquarters announced that it would remain neutral during the campaign rather than back the prime minister's stance."

It was a Conservative Party manifesto commitment to offer "an in-out referendum by the end of 2017".

| *The Times* | **Reversed pictures and** | 19 Jan 16 |
| *Feedback* | **barbecued duck** | |

Rose,
I fear that your note about which side medals are supposed to go may not have got through to the picture staff, in one sense or the other. See the screenshot, below, of Lord Bramall on Saturday. Also, I wonder if you have received any explanation from the editor of the relevant section about the barbecued duck recipe.

See pages 191/192 and 197/198.
No reply!

| *Private Eye* | **Commentatorballs** | 21 Jan 16 |

"You take those opportunities, they stick in that one-handed spectacular catch, and momentum swings completely on its head."
MARCUS TRESCOTHICK, Sky Sports

| *The Cricketer* | **Obituaries** | 26 Jan 16 |

I am about to enter my fortieth year as a subscriber, during which time I have seen the magazine develop and expand enormously in the way that it both informs and entertains. But it also a record, so may I make a plea about the handling of obituaries: that a photograph is included, however small, with all of them. Less than half had this treatment last year; so far this year only one out six has a photograph. Of course space is a factor, but so too I imagine is the effort to source photographs. If someone warrants an obituary in *The Cricketer*, then readers and researchers expect nowadays to find with it a likeness of them, whether in their prime or otherwise.

We have noted your comments,   26 Jan 16
with thanks Malcolm.
As you say, sometimes it's tricky to source pictures, but on occasion a contributor will send a pic in to accompany their words.
Anyhow, we will try harder in future.
Many thanks for being with us for 40 years!
Here's to the half-century.
Best, Huw Turbervill

I cannot recall if I have replied Malcolm.   4 Feb 16
I believe I did.
But just to say I forwarded this on to our designers.
As I think I said, it does depend on availability of pictures, if someone sends one in etc, but we have noted your remarks and will try to act upon them.
Thanks for reading!

Dear Huw,   16 Feb 16

You did reply but thank you for the additional information. My point is that it should be editorial policy to have a picture with each obituary you publish. It will not happen if the matter is devolved to your designers. Also, the message will soon get through to those offering them: no picture, no obituary.

Malcolm,   23 Feb 16
Agreed that we will try to have a picture with every obit from now on.
Thanks for your interest.
Best wishes, Huw

The Times   **Graphical exaggeration**   29 Feb 16
Feedback

Dear Rose,
As we enter the second week of Project Fear may I make a plea for *The Times* to take a lead and not enhance the scaremongering by further exaggeration in its use of graphics. This is done in graphs by truncating the y axis so that it does not start at zero, as below, giving the impression of much greater changes than actually exist.

I accept that this has been in general use for years, as shown from the business pages in the second screenshot below, but it is vitally important that claims by both sides in the EU referendum debate are not exaggerated in this way as the vast majority will not be versed in these deceptions.

The easiest way to correct this for a simple graph or histogram (bar) is for there to be a small jagged line at the start of the y axis, where it does not start at zero. Other examples and the impact of this are shown in the screenshot at the bottom.

I can imagine that such an initiative would benefit from agreement across the press and, if used, may also require an explanation or warning during the run up to the vote, hence my plea for you to take a lead.

The Cricketer   **April issue – letters page**   17 Mar 16

Sir,

> Obituaries with photos - that's much better,
> But whatever happened to my letter?
> **Donning the right pullover** is there in bold,
> Beneath it a different story has been told.

See pages 144/145 and 199-201.

Malcolm,   18 Mar 16
I see what you mean.
Not sure what happened there. Sorry about that.
Should have been **Syria's cricket connection** *or some such.*
I'll put the letter through the system again.
Glad you are pleased about the obits, however.
Best, Huw

The Times	**Hyperlinks**	24 Mar 16
Feedback		

Dear Rose,

The practice of providing hyperlinks on the website has been reducing and now seems to have stopped, notably in the letters. Please can this timesaving device be reintroduced wherever references (in brackets) are displayed.

No reply, though the links were restored two days later, only to drop out again. On 30 March, a new website was launched with no sign of any hyperlinks.

To be continued…

YET MORE
LAST WORDS

"For my part, I travel not to go anywhere, but to go. I travel for travel's sake. The great affair is to move."

Robert Louis Stevenson, *Travels with a Donkey* (1879)

ACKNOWLEDGEMENTS

This book has been self-published, the third time I have done so using lulu.com and so help needed is minimised. I am most grateful though to Martyn Ezra for his encouragement and help in converting the volumes to e-books on Amazon Kindle, work in progress at the time of publication.

Special thanks are due to Michael Bromley Gardner, whose eagle eye for spotting typos and errors has eliminated the need for any other proofreaders.

I am also indebted to three more acknowledged exponents of the written word in their respective fields for their enticing forewords and to another, Martin Johnson, the sports journalist, for his ringing endorsement on the back cover.

Last, my grateful thanks go to the renowned cartoonist, Bill Tidy, for his picture on the front cover and his continued interest in my endeavours, which could yet break new ground in the future.

ABOUT THE SUBJECT

Malcolm Watson was born in Beverley in the East Riding of Yorkshire and educated at Oundle and the Royal Military Academy Sandhurst, being commissioned into The Queen's Own Hussars; and at the Royal Military College of Science Shrivenham, from where he obtained a degree in Aeromechanical Engineering. He was in the Army for 39 years, serving at various times in England and Northern Ireland, and abroad in Cyprus, Hong Kong, West Germany, West Berlin, Washington DC and Mexico City, where as the defence attaché he was also accredited to Belize and Cuba. He has made 10 military parachute jumps and flown 35 hours in a Piper Cherokee. He played and watched more cricket than was thought possible for a serviceman; he has been a member of Yorkshire County Cricket Club for over 50 years and MCC for 37. He enjoys acting the fool and has taken part in a number of reviews on stage and elsewhere. His only serious and non-speaking part, to date, was playing King George lV at his Coronation in the Berlin Military Tattoo. He is interested in everything except classical music, Shakespeare and Greek mythology. He is married to Jane and they have 3 daughters, Anna, Edwina and Fenella.

"…he will speak his mind whenever the occasion warrants it (and perhaps some when it does not!)…"
Extract from a Regular Army Confidential Report